# Czech Republic

# Czech Republic

**BY LURA ROGERS SEAVEY**

*Enchantment of the World*™
*Second Series*

**CHILDREN'S PRESS**®

An Imprint of Scholastic Inc.

Frontispiece: **Cesky Krumlov**

*Consultant:* Kirsten Lodge, Associate Professor of Humanities and English, Midwestern State University, Wichita Falls, Texas

*Please note: All statistics are as up-to-date as possible at the time of publication.*

Book production by The Design Lab

Library of Congress Cataloging-in-Publication Data
Names: Rogers Seavey, Lura, author.
Title: Czech Republic / by Lura Rogers Seavey.
Description: New York : Children's Press, an Imprint of Scholastic Inc., [2018] | Series:
   Enchantment of the world | Includes bibliographical references and index.
Identifiers: LCCN 2017025776 | ISBN 9780531235898 (library binding)
Subjects: LCSH: Czech Republic—Juvenile literature.
Classification: LCC DB2011 .R65 2018 | DDC 943.71—dc23
LC record available at https://lccn.loc.gov/2017025776

Scholastic Inc., 557 Broadway, New York, NY 10012

1 2 3 4 5 6 7 8 9 10 R 27 26 25 24 23 22 21 20 19 18

**Astronomical clock, Prague**

# Contents

*Left to right:* **Folk dancing, forest, St. Vitus Cathedral, painting a building in Prague, Carnival celebration**

# CHAPTER 1

# Welcome to Czechia

8

THE CZECH REPUBLIC IS A PROUD NATION THAT HAS overcome adversity time after time during its long history. Located in the center of Europe, Czechia, as it is often called, serves as a gateway between eastern and western Europe. The country's landscape is beautiful, with deep chasms, limestone caves, and towering rock formations carved by rain and wind.

Czech history is the story of a land tested by conflict and oppression. Regional powers have competed for control of the area, and Catholics and Protestants have battled for power and freedom. In 1918, Czechoslovakia emerged as an independent nation, encompassing what are now the Czech Republic and Slovakia. After a mere two decades of independence, however, Czechoslovakia was invaded by German forces in 1939, and it remained occupied by Germans

*Opposite:* **Many cities across the Czech Republic have well-preserved historic centers, with buildings that date back hundreds of years.**

throughout World War II. The end of the war brought a different kind of oppression, as a brutal communist regime took hold. But the Czech people refused to give up. After decades of suffering, they fought for democracy, and in 1989, the communists were ousted.

Today's Czech Republic is a mix of the old and the new. Its capital city, Prague, has remarkable historic sites, a charming old medieval center, and endless neighborhoods with winding streets. Many people consider Prague one of the most beautiful cities in the world. It is one of the most visited cities in the world, as well as a center of finance, technology, and education. Outside of Prague, in the cities and villages alike, you will find old traditions preserved next to new industries and modern ways. You will find a resilient people, and a country that is getting stronger. Come explore the Czech Republic.

**Prague is a vibrant mix of old and new.**

# CHAPTER 2

# Cradled by Mountains

THE CZECH REPUBLIC IS A MODEST-SIZED COUNTRY, slightly smaller than the U.S. state of North Carolina. Lying in the middle of Europe, it is completely landlocked. Germany lies to the west, Poland to the northeast, Slovakia to the southeast, and Austria to the south.

The Czech Republic is divided into three cultural regions. The largest of these is Bohemia, which lies in the west and makes up more than one-half of the country. The next largest is Moravia, which occupies most of the eastern Czech Republic, while Czech Silesia lies along the northeastern border.

## In the Mountains

Several different mountain ranges rise along the border of the northern part of the Czech Republic. The Jested Ridge sits at the country's northernmost point. Nearby are the Jizera

*Opposite:* **A hiker enjoys a fabulous view from Klet, a mountain near Cesky Krumlov in southern Bohemia.**

## Czechia's Geographic Features

**Area:** 30,450 square miles (78,865 sq km)

**Highest Elevation:** Mount Snezka, 5,256 feet (1,602 m) above sea level

**Lowest Elevation:** Village of Hrensko, 377 feet (115 m) above sea level

**Longest River:** Vltava, 267 miles (430 km)

**Largest Lake:** Black Lake, 45 acres (18 ha)

**Largest Reservoir:** Lipno, 19 square miles (49 sq km)

**Longest Natural Cave System:** Koneprusy Caves, 1.2 miles (2 km)

**Average High Temperature:** In Prague, 34°F (1°C) in January, 76°F (24°C) in July

**Average Low Temperature:** In Prague, 25°F (−4°C) in January, 55°F (13°C) in July

**Average Annual Precipitation:** 18 to 60 inches (45 to 150 cm), depending on location

Mountains. A protected area, the Jizera Mountains are a popular spot for skiing and other winter sports. They extend southeast into the Giant Mountains (Krkonose in Czech). The Giant Mountains are home to the country's tallest peak, Mount Snezka, which rises to 5,256 feet (1,602 meters) above sea level. As the border turns sharply south, the Eagle Mountains begin, creating Bohemia's northeastern border with Poland. The Broumov region, famous for its spectacular rock cities, sits along the northern part of the range.

**The rock formations in northern Bohemia have been attracting tourists since the nineteenth century.**

## What Is Karst?

Caves in the Czech Republic are often referred to as karst caves. Karst is not a type of stone. Instead, it refers to porous rock that has been worn away by water. Most karst regions have bedrock made of limestone, gypsum, sandstone, or dolomite. These types of rock are easily dissolved by acidic water.

Caves are formed in karst regions by water running underground, eroding paths along the way. This water may come from natural springs, or it could be rainwater or runoff that has seeped down through a crack in the soft bedrock. In some places, entire rivers disappear into underground channels when they burrow into the soft stone.

Along with caves, sinkholes are common in karst regions. Here the earth has collapsed in on itself because the cave beneath cannot support it. One of the best known is the flooded Hranice Abyss, whose exact

depth is still unknown. A diving research robot has gone to a depth of 1,325 feet (404 meters) and still not hit the bottom. The Macocha Abyss, which is 453 feet (138 m) deep, is a popular tourist site.

Karst topography can also create some beautiful aboveground features as parts of the stone are washed away by rain. The more soluble parts erode leaving the denser rock behind to form natural sculptures. The Czechs refer to groupings of these formations as "rock cities" because they look like a skyline—tall rock towers jutting out of the earth side by side. The Prachov Rock Formations in northwestern Bohemia and the Hruboskalsko sandstone city are two of the biggest, and are part of protected nature reserves to ensure that many generations can marvel at their awesome beauty.

**The Punkva River flows through the Moravian Karst region. It is underground much of the time, carving out caves, but it emerges in the Macocha Abyss.**

The Jesenik Mountains lie in the east, along the border with Poland. The many streams flowing down from the mountains give this area fertile farmland. Here you can find the impressive Hranice Abyss, the world's deepest known flooded cave. In the southeast, along the border with Slovakia, are the Beskid and White Carpathian Mountains.

In the southeast is a region called the Bohemian-Moravian Highlands. This elevated area includes a spectacular region called the Moravian Karst. This region is home to more than a thousand caves and many breathtaking gorges, including the Macocha Abyss. Brno, the country's second-largest city, is in this area.

## Hidden Wonders

The Czech Republic has three distinct regions of karst landscape, which are riddled with several thousand caves. Most are in the eastern part of the country, particularly central Moravia. The most concentrated group is a 36-square-mile (93 square kilometers) protected nature reserve known as the Moravian Karst. It includes impressive gorges and many natural cave systems, five of which are open to the public.

Moravia's caves may be plentiful, but the largest single cave system in the Czech Republic is located near Prague. The Koneprusy Caves are the longest and deepest known caves in the country, stretching 1.2 miles (2 km) and reaching 230 feet (70 m) belowground. Visitors can explore the passages and chambers, keeping an eye out for a phenomenon called the Koneprusy Roses. These unique formations were created long ago as the dissolved calcium carbonate from the eroding rocks above seeped down and rehardened into bush-like shapes. Over time, some of the minerals wore away again, leaving behind formations that resemble rose blossoms.

In the southwest of the country, along the German border, are the massive Sumava Mountains. Most of this area is protected as the Sumava National Park. This park protects the largest forest in central Europe, along with lakes, bogs, and abundant wildlife.

The Ore Mountains extend along the entire northwestern border of the Czech Republic, separating it from Germany. This region is rich in minerals, especially lignite coal deposits. Mining has caused extensive environmental damage

## To Health!

At the westernmost point of the Czech Republic along the German border is the city of Karlovy Vary. Thanks to its active geology, a major industry in Karlovy Vary is medicinal spas. Waters in the natural springs in the region are filled with minerals, which are believed to cure many ailments. People come to Karlovy Vary to drink the mineral waters and soak in the hot springs.

that has left the landscape scarred and contaminated and the air polluted from the many coal-burning power plants. Despite this, the region is popular with tourists who come

**Pink wildflowers brighten a meadow near the forest in Sumava National Park.**

to see its many beautiful natural sites, particularly Bohemian Switzerland National Park. This park features beautiful mountains, weather-worn canyons, and many rock cities, or groups of towering sandstone formations. It also boasts Europe's largest sandstone arch, which is 52 feet (16 m) high and 26 feet (8 m) wide.

In the middle of the Czech Republic, surrounded by all these mountain ranges, is a region called the Bohemian Massif. This is an area of rolling hills and valleys.

**A massive sandstone arch is the best-known site in Bohemian Switzerland National Park. Because of erosion, visitors are no longer allowed to climb on it.**

## A Look at Czech Cities

The largest city in the Czech Republic is its capital, Prague, which has a population of 1,165,581. Brno (right) is the second-largest city in the Czech Republic, with a population of 369,559. Lying in the southeast, it is the symbolic capital of the historical region of Moravia. Although Prague is the national capital, the Czech government did not want it to have too much official power, so the highest courts in the land are based in Brno. Both the Supreme Court and the Constitutional Court are located there. Brno is also a center of the technology industry, especially software development and communications. Many tourists travel to Brno to visit its historic sites, such as Spilberk Castle, which was built in the thirteenth century. Another attractive building is the Cathedral of Sts. Peter and Paul, which was built starting in the fourteenth century.

Ostrava, with a population of 313,088, sits near the Polish border. The surrounding area has many mines, and steel production has been dominant there since the early 1800s. The massive Vitkovice ironworks complex in the center of the city is an icon of the industry,

described by many as looking like it should be in a science fiction story because of its towering steel structures. A unique spot nearby is the Ema slag heap, an artificial hill that is actually a giant pile of waste from the coal mines. Deep below the surface, the discarded mine slag is burning, and smoke can be seen escaping cracks in the earth. This constant heat keeps the hill warm year-round, creating a subtropical microclimate where flowers grow in the dead of winter.

Pilsen (left) is a picturesque city, the fourth-largest city in the Czech Republic, with a population 164,180. It is internationally known as the home of the Pilsner Urquell Brewery and the birthplace of the Pilsner variety of beer. The majestic St. Bartholomew's Cathedral has the tallest church spire in the country, and the city's synagogue (Jewish house of worship) is the second largest in Europe. Underneath the city's historic district hides a network of medieval tunnels and cellars.

Olomouc, with a population 101,268, is located in Moravia. The city lies on the Morava River and was built on the site of what was once a Roman fort. Today, it is home to Palacky University, one of the nation's largest, and is often filled with students. The city's most prominent sites include the Cathedral of St. Wenceslas and the Holy Trinity Column, erected in the city center after the plague swept through in the early 1700s.

**The Elbe and Vltava Rivers flow together at Melnik, north of Prague.**

## Rivers and Lakes

Many rivers and streams originate in the mountains of the Czech Republic. The longest of these is the Vltava, which stretches 267 miles (430 kilometers) within Czech borders. It rises along the border with Germany, runs across Bohemia and through the capital city of Prague before feeding into the Elbe River.

The Elbe River, the country's second-longest, does not travel as far as the Vltava, but carries more water. It originates in the Giant Mountains along the Polish border. All along its route, it is fed by smaller streams and merges with other rivers, eventually becoming a major waterway that flows through Germany and empties into the North Sea.

Because of the Czech Republic's extremely porous bedrock, water seeps into the land rather than staying on the surface, so there are few natural lakes or ponds. For at least the past six hundred years, the Czech people have been creating artificial ponds, many of which are still in use today. With modern technology, reservoirs formed by dams have created large lakes for fishing, recreation, and drinking water. The biggest of these is Lipno, on the Vltava River in the southwest. Of the few natural lakes, Black Lake in the Sumava Mountains is the largest.

**Czechs enjoy the cool water of Lipno Lake on a warm summer day.**

## Climate

The Czech Republic's climate is generally moderate. There are four distinct seasons, with warm summers averaging above 70 degrees Fahrenheit (21 degrees Celsius) and cool winters with temperatures usually dipping to below freezing. Because buildings usually hold on to heat, the city of Prague often reaches much higher temperatures than the national average, especially in the summer. The higher elevations experience colder temperatures year-round.

Precipitation varies across the country, with central Bohemia averaging as little as 18 inches (45 centimeters) of rain a year,

**Snowfall is common during the winter in Prague.**

while some mountainous regions receive 60 inches (150 cm). In much of the country, rainfall is most common during the summer.

Emissions rise from a coal-burning power plant in northern Bohemia. Many Czech power plants have been modernized, so they release fewer harmful pollutants.

## Environmental Concerns

Throughout most of the twentieth century, natural resources in the Czech Republic were exploited with little concern for the environment. Mining left the landscape torn and polluted the water. By the 1990s, the pollutants emitted by coal-burning power plants and factories had given the nation the world's highest levels of carbon dioxide emissions. In recent decades, however, the Czech government has paid more attention to the environment. The Czech Republic has established several environmental protection organizations and designated protected natural areas. Although factory emissions have declined, air pollution remains a problem.

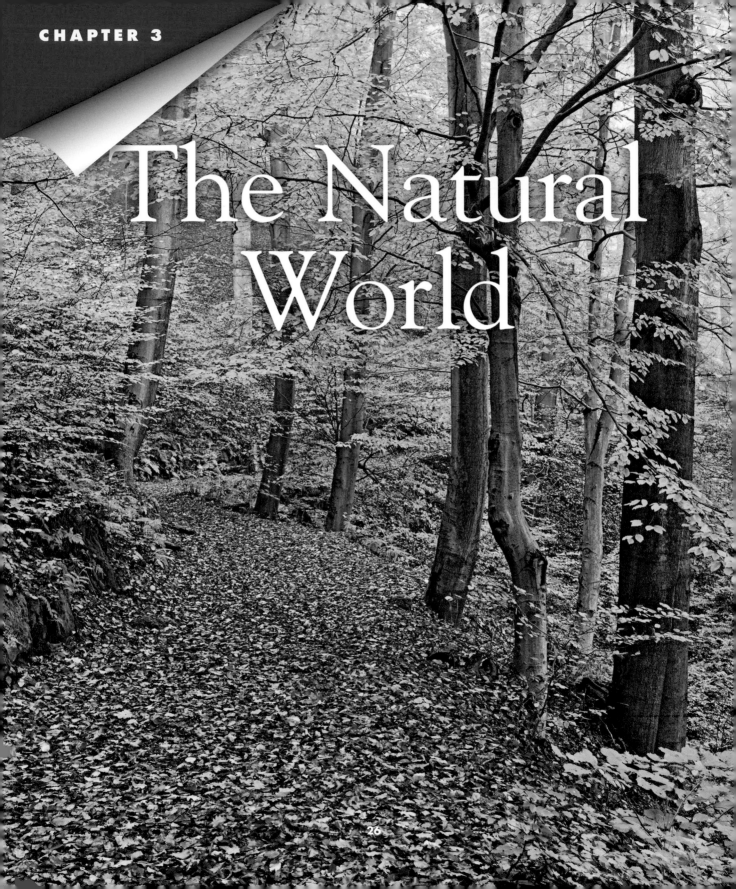

# CHAPTER 3

# The Natural World

**T**HE CZECH REPUBLIC'S PLANT AND ANIMAL LIFE is as varied as its landscape. Although human activity has caused some species to become rare, many creatures continue to thrive.

*Opposite:* **About a third of the land in the Czech Republic is covered in forest.**

## Plant Life

The trees that grow in the Czech Republic vary with elevation. Oak and beech occupy the lowest zones, while spruce and fir are more common at higher elevations. Most of the abundant spruce trees were planted to replace trees that were harvested for timber and fuel.

The timberline, the point at which the elevation is too high for trees to grow, sits at approximately 4,500 feet (1,400 m) above sea level. At elevations above the timberline, low bushes and grasses thrive.

## Mammals

The Czech Republic is home to several different species of large mammals. Red deer are plentiful in the forests and uninhabited areas of the country. European elk, called moose in North America, are found in forests and wetlands of the lower, more temperate elevations. In northern Moravia, small populations of lynx, wolves, and bears roam the hills and forests. They are slowly increasing in number.

Smaller creatures, such as minks and otters, live near rivers and streams. These species have suffered from overhunting, and their numbers are still recovering. Hares and rabbits thrive in most Czech regions, while squirrel-like alpine marmots and

weasel-like martens live at higher altitudes. The European polecat, which looks and behaves very much like its cousin the ferret, can be found anywhere there is a rodent population.

European polecats are excellent hunters, stalking creatures as varied as voles, frogs, and birds.

### Bats: Overcoming a Bad Rap

With its thousands of caves, it is no surprise that the Czech Republic is home to more than two dozen species of bat. As a result, the region has plenty of bat-related stories and superstitions.

Although many people regard them as a pest or are afraid of them, bats are an important part of the ecosystem and they help control insect populations. In 1991, the Czech Bat Conservation Trust was established to oversee research and ensure conservation of bats and their habitat. The organization also works to increase awareness about the species and dispel myths that make them considered an unpopular neighbor.

Common bat varieties in the Czech Republic are the brown long-eared bat (left), the northern bat, and the pond bat. Others include the noctule bat, the whiskered bat, and the greater mouse-eared bat.

## In the Air

The Czech Republic is home to a large population of game birds, those that are hunted for sport or food. Ducks are common near water, pheasants and partridges roam the countryside, and wild geese fill the sky. Rarer large birds, such as the heron and the eagle, are protected species. With patience and some luck, visitors may also be able to spot owls, storks, and vultures. Fish-eating birds eat many of the carp that are stocked in the country's reservoirs and ponds.

**Hundreds of species of birds live in the Czech Republic. These include swans, which often swim in the Vltava River in Prague, hoping to be fed by visitors.**

## The White Deer of Bohemia

The extremely rare white deer did not originate in the Czech Republic, but it is now one of the only places in the world it can be found. White deer are not albinos, which lack all pigment and have dark pink eyes. Instead, they are a unique species with white fur and usually brilliant blue eyes.

Some wealthy people introduced the deer into the region in the 1780s. The population dwindled, and in less than fifty years only a few remained. They were given to Count Matthias Thun-Hohenstein of Zehusice, in eastern Bohemia. He cared for them and their numbers increased slightly, but by the 1940s, there were barely over two dozen left. Interbreeding threatened their health, so in the 1970s a second herd was formed and they were interbred with the closely related red deer. There are now four Czech sanctuaries for these deer, which together currently have a population of almost three hundred.

## Rare and Protected

Both private and government organizations help protect vulnerable plants and animals and help them recover from past damage done by the overuse of land and by pollution. Nature reserves have been established in the Jizera Mountains, the Sumava Forest, and the Moravian Karst. Krkonose National Park specifically protects its unique alpine terrain and the creatures that live there, such as the alpine shrew. A type of large wild sheep called a mouflon has also been introduced into these mountainous reserves.

# CHAPTER 4

# The Long Road

**L**IVING IN A SMALL COUNTRY SITTING RIGHT IN the center of Europe, the Czech people have sometimes been at the mercy of the regional powers that have taken over large parts of the continent. At times when a Czech national identity began to thrive, oppressive foreign rulers took over the land. The Czech Republic now stands as a proud reminder that freedom is always worth the fight.

## Early People

The first evidence of human settlement in what is now the Czech Republic dates back at least thirty thousand years. These earliest people were hunters and gatherers. They made tools from bones and stone and made art, shaping figures from clay and tusks.

More than two thousand years ago, a Celtic tribe called the Boii settled in the region. The Celts were an ancient people who spread across much of Europe and the British Isles. The Boii were the source of the name Bohemia.

*Opposite:* **The Crown of St. Wenceslas is part of the Bohemian crown jewels. It was made in 1346 for the coronation of Charles IV.**

## Prehistoric Discoveries

In 1884, archaeologists discovered a site called Predmosti in central Moravia. They found evidence of two settlements dating back to between 27,000 and 24,000 BCE. These artifacts are important in understanding early human development. They reveal a great deal about the way of life of early humans.

The remains of over one thousand mammoths—large, elephant-like creatures—have been uncovered in the area. They were a main source of food for these early people, who used the huge bones to make tools and build structures. Bones were also used to create decorative items like figurines. Ivory from mammoth tusks was carved into decorative items and engraved with intricate patterns and shapes (right).

At the Predmosti site, archaeologists also uncovered the skulls of three dogs. These skulls have specific characteristics that indicate that they were not wolves. Instead, they had been domesticated animals—in other words, pets. One of the dogs was even buried with a mammoth bone placed in its mouth!

## Enter the Slavs

Eventually, the Germanic Marcomanni and Quidi tribes pushed the Celts out. They remained for nearly a thousand years until they were edged out in the late fifth century CE when large groups of Slavs migrated from the east.

The Slavs are the ancestors of many of today's eastern Europeans, including people of the Czech Republic, Slovakia, Poland, Ukraine, and Russia. They lived for over a century as independent tribes, and eventually united against a common enemy, the Avar Empire, which was based to the southeast. This union is referred to as Samo's Kingdom, named for the leader who helped them organize.

Around the year 830 CE, the Great Moravian Empire was built by a leader named Mojmir. It spread into the areas that are now Slovakia, Bohemia, and parts of Hungary and Poland.

## The Premyslid Years

Meanwhile, the Hungarian Premyslid dynasty had already begun growing roots in Moravia, and its rulers were preparing to expand. In 880, Prince Borivoj built Prague Castle, and gradually Premyslid royalty began to establish important positions as the existing government faltered. In the year 907, the Hungarians invaded Moravia, and the Moravian Empire fell.

The Premyslid dynasty lasted for four centuries, and during this time the region began to form its own identity as the Czech state. The new leaders were Roman Catholic, which meant that politically they were tied to the Holy Roman Empire, a powerful Germanic empire in central Europe that had the support of the

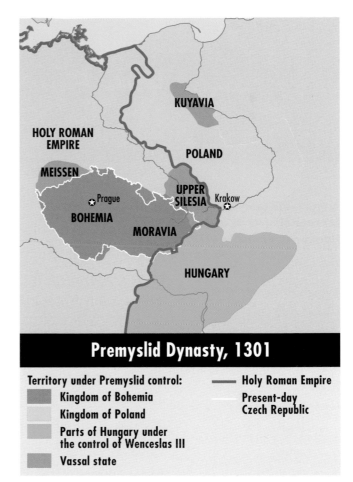

**Premyslid Dynasty, 1301**

Territory under Premyslid control:
- Kingdom of Bohemia
- Kingdom of Poland
- Parts of Hungary under the control of Wenceslas III
- Vassal state

—— Holy Roman Empire
—— Present-day Czech Republic

**A Premyslid army battles for control of lands under Hungarian control in 1278.**

Catholic Church, based in Rome. Unlike many parts of the Holy Roman Empire, the Premyslid dynasty was able to hold on to self-rule. Support for the Church was important, however, because of the vast power and influence that it held. The establishment of the Prague Bishopric in the late 900s made Prague the seat of a high-ranking official in the Church. The bishop resided in the castle with Premyslid leaders and was influential in all political decisions. In 1085, the Church allowed Prince Vratislav to use a formal royal title, and he became the first official Czech king.

In the year 1212, a decree called the Golden Bull of Sicily was issued by the Holy Roman Empire. This officially rec-

Wenceslas I was part of the Premyslid dynasty, and ruled as duke of Bohemia from 922 until 935. After he was forced to give tribute to a German king, some noblemen began conspiring against him. They encouraged his jealous younger brother Boleslav to kill him. Wenceslas, who was renowned for his Christian beliefs, was on his way to mass when Boleslav attacked him, killing him in front of the church.

While in power, Wenceslas was known for his reasonable policies and for ending the persecution of Christians that his mother had imposed while she ruled during his childhood. He was also highly educated, an excellent negotiator, and respected by his subjects.

Following his murder, he was thought of as a martyr—someone who is killed for his or her religious beliefs—and became an important symbol to Czech Christians. He was eventually named a saint and given the honorary title of king. Since then, he has been considered the patron saint of the Czech people.

ognized the hereditary lineage of the Premyslid royal family, ensuring that the Church would support the family's claim to the throne throughout the generations. This decree also bonded the Bohemians to the Holy Roman Empire, giving the Church full control of Bohemia.

The Premyslid bloodline ended with the murder of King Wenceslas III in 1306. The Luxembourg royal family was prepared to step in at this opportunity. John of Luxembourg married the sister of Wenceslas III, becoming the new king of Bohemia in 1310.

### The Golden Age of Prague

Upon John of Luxembourg's death in 1346, his son Charles came to power. He would reign for thirty-two years as Charles IV. These years are sometimes called Prague's Golden Age because of his successful rule.

Charles IV was well educated and fascinated with the arts and sciences. He welcomed scholars to his court and in 1348 founded the first university in central Europe, known today as Charles University. As the importance of Prague grew, so did its landscape. During his rule, the Charles Bridge and

Charles IV is considered the father of the Czech Republic, and Prague flourished during his reign. Many sites in the city are now named after him, including the Charles Bridge and Charles University.

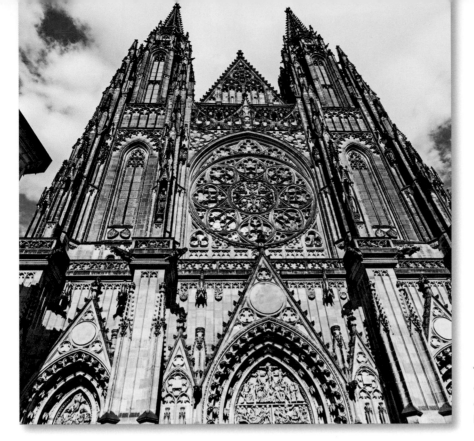

The soaring main tower of St. Vitus Cathedral is as tall as a thirty-story building.

several castles were constructed, and St. Vitus Cathedral was rebuilt. Grand examples of gothic architecture sprang up all over Prague, and the city's population increased. Additionally, Charles IV was an experienced and skilled diplomat, and his greatest accomplishment came in 1355 when he was crowned the Emperor of the Holy Roman Empire, and declared Prague the capital city.

## The Hussite Revolution

When Charles died in 1378, King Wenceslas IV took over the throne. The Roman Catholic Church was extremely wealthy and focused many of its resources on gaining land, riches, and power throughout its empire. Over time, the overworked and

In 1500, Prague was home to an estimated seventy thousand people. The castle dominated the city below.

overtaxed masses began to question this, and many believed that the Church had become greedy, straying far from the Christian principles of charity. One of the most outspoken opponents of the wealth, power, and corruption of the Catholic Church was a professor at Charles University named Jan Hus. Soon, Hus's followers included not only students at the university but also a significant portion of Prague's population.

Questioning the teachings of the Church was heresy—meaning one's beliefs were in violation of religious doctrines. The Pope, the leader of the Roman Catholic Church, was furious. To punish those who protested Church practice, he banned them from taking part in any official church

## The Spark of a Revolution

Jan Hus was born in the town of Husinec in southern Bohemia around the year 1370. By the time he was thirty, he was a dean at the University of Prague.

At this time, the Roman Catholic Church had nearly limitless power in the region. It owned about half the land in Bohemia. Hus recognized that the extreme wealth of the Church and its clergy was hurting Bohemians, in large part because the Church imposed high taxes on the people.

Hus became active in trying to change Church practice. He spoke out, preaching at the Bethlehem Chapel in Prague in 1402. His sermons were in Czech, rather than in Latin as Church proceedings normally were.

When the Church threatened to punish all of Prague's residents for Hus's outspoken views, Hus went into exile. During this time, he continued to write and express his views.

In 1414, King Sigismund of Hungary invited Hus to present his views at an official Church council. Although Hus knew it was a trap, he had no choice but to go. He was imprisoned soon after his arrival and subjected to a long trial. Hus believed so strongly in his views that he refused to back down, and he was sentenced to death for heresy. He was burned at the stake on July 6, 1415. He became a martyr for the reform movement, and the Hussite Revolution was named in his honor.

ceremonies, including marriage, baptism, and funerals. Because the government and the Church were one entity, it meant that even if a priest could be bribed to perform the rites for those who had been banned, they would not be recognized or legal.

On July 6, 1415, Jan Hus was burned at the stake for the crime of heresy. Church officials believed that this would scare his disciples into silence and end their objections. Instead, it made them more determined than ever to stop the Church from abusing its power. Hus became a martyr for reform efforts, and this widespread movement was eventually named for him—the Hussite Revolution.

At his trial for heresy in 1415, Jan Hus refused to recant, or admit he was wrong. When he was taken to the execution grounds he again refused to recant, and he was burned at the stake.

**Hussites throw a city official out the window of the New Town Hall in 1419. Seven officials were killed in the attack.**

The Hussite Revolution lasted from 1419 to 1436. It was officially launched by a group led by preacher Jan Zelivsky when his group overthrew the government council—in part literally. On July 30, 1419, a group of Hussites raided the New Town Hall in Prague and tossed the officials out the windows, killing them all. The event is known as the First Defenestration of Prague. (*Defenestration* means "the throwing of someone out a window," *fenestre* being Latin for "window.") The Church punished Prague and known Hussite regions by banning them from trade. These new embargo laws left residents unable to get supplies or sell their goods to outsiders to make money. During the difficult years of the Hussite Revolution, many Bohemians died of starvation and illness because of the stalled economy.

**Jan Zizka was a military genius who never lost a battle.**

The Holy Roman Emperor Sigismund launched five crusades against the Hussites, but each time he failed. One reason the Hussites endured was because of their military leader, Jan Zizka. His strategies and management of troops were unlike those of any commander before him. He mounted cannons on wagons. When a cavalry—soldiers on horseback—attacked, his men would use the fortified wagons as a wall. From behind the wagons, they would shoot muskets and cannons to disable the horses, weakening the strongest troops first. As a result of such innovations, he never lost a battle during his career and revolutionized military strategy.

Eventually, differences arose among the Hussites, and they split into a number of groups. Some were more extreme in their beliefs than others. The moderate Hussites were known as Utraquists or Praguers. The Taborites were much stricter in their beliefs and did not want to compromise at all. Jan Zizka's followers were also a radical group, taking the name the Orphans after Zizka's death.

Eventually, Sigismund realized that he could not win against the Hussites, so in October 1431, negotiations in what is called the Council of Basel began in hopes of finding compromise. It was a slow process, and during this time the fighting continued. The moderates were desperate to find middle ground and end the fighting. In 1434, moderate Hussites joined forces with Catholics and succeeded in defeating the Taborites at the Battle of Lipany. Finally, in 1436, the negotiators at Basel came to an agreement and signed a contract called the Compacts of Basel.

## Enter the Habsburgs

This marked the first time in history that the Catholic Church allowed another faith to be practiced in a territory under its dominion. In 1452, the moderate Hussite George of Podebrady was elected governor of the Bohemian assembly, and in 1458 he became the king of Bohemia. His reign was remarkable for his attention to diplomacy. He tried to bring together European leaders in an official, cooperative union, much like today's United Nations. He mended international relationships, but domestic politics were still unstable. Czech Catholics did not support a Hussite ruler, and the Hungarian monarchy wanted his throne. Before his death, George of Podebrady made an agreement with the Jagiellon line of Polish royalty, giving them succession of his throne. The Jagiellon dynasty lasted only from 1471 until 1526, when there were no further heirs. This gave the powerful Austrian Habsburg family the opportunity to expand its dynasty.

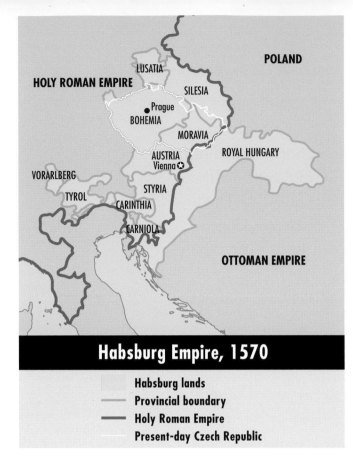

## Habsburg Empire, 1570

Habsburg lands
Provincial boundary
Holy Roman Empire
Present-day Czech Republic

Ferdinand I of Habsburg immediately reinstated Catholicism as the official religion. Prague lost its importance when Vienna became the new seat of power for the empire. It was not until the rule of Rudolf II, from 1576 to 1611, that Prague regained its importance—and saw its second Golden Age. In 1583, the royal court was moved back to Prague, and with this Prague's cultural and political importance grew. Rudolf became an important patron of art and science, and during his reign, Prague became a highly respected intellectual center once more.

When Rudolf's brother Matthias took the throne in 1611, he immediately began to oppress the Protestants. In 1618, Protestants raided Prague Castle in what is known as the Second Defenestration of Prague. They, too, tossed government officials out the window—although this time the victims were lucky enough to land in a pile of trash and survive.

The Battle of White Mountain in 1620 marked the beginning of the Thirty Years' War, a war fought across central Europe among the Habsburgs, their allies, and their enemies over religion, land, and family dynasties. To show their power, the Habsburgs executed more than two dozen Protestant leaders in Prague's Old Town Square in June 1621. The govern-

### The King and His Court

Rudolf II was born in 1552 in Vienna, and when he took the throne, that's where the royal court was based. But Rudolf suffered from depression, so in 1583, he moved the court back to Prague because he believed he could live a quieter life there.

This move increased Prague's stature as a center of culture. The king had a deep interest in art and science. He became a great patron of the arts, and it is said he would gaze at paintings for hours at a time. He was just as fascinated by science. He collected scientific instruments, gemstones, minerals, feathers, fossils, manuscripts, and much more. The dozens of cabinets required to store and display his massive collection took up several rooms.

Rudolf especially revered astronomers. He welcomed two of the greatest scientists of the age, Tycho Brahe from Denmark and Johannes Kepler from Germany, to his court (above). There they did some of their groundbreaking work, studying the movement of the stars and planets.

Although Rudolf II did much to promote art and science during his reign, he was less adept at governing his empire. As he grew older, his mental state grew worse, and by 1605, his family had forced him to give up some control to his brother Matthias. Six years later, Matthias's army held Rudolf prisoner in his castle in Prague until he agreed to give Matthias control of Bohemia. After this, Rudolf still held the title Holy Roman Emperor, but it came with no power. He died the following year.

ment imposed new laws that banned any religion other than Catholicism, and Protestants were forced to leave the country if they would not convert. Many aspects of Czech culture were discouraged or banned, including the Czech language. During this time, the Habsburgs also staked a hereditary claim to the throne of Bohemia, ensuring the family's lasting rule.

In the eighteenth century, Queen Maria Theresa and her son Joseph II brought reforms that lifted the oppressive religious restrictions. During this period of enlightenment,

**Swedish soldiers enter Prague in 1648 on their way to capturing Prague Castle. The Battle of Prague was the last battle of the Thirty Years' War.**

the direct power of the Catholic Church began to recede. In 1781, Joseph II's Edict of Toleration gave Protestants some limited freedom of worship. They could follow their own religions but could not build obvious church buildings. The following year Joseph issued a second edict, which ended some discrimination against Jews. They were now allowed to attend universities and enter more occupations.

This period also brought the reestablishment of the rights of both Bohemia and Moravia, granting them some independence within the Habsburg Empire.

Maria Theresa with her son Joseph II. A dominant figure in eighteenth-century Europe, she was the only female ruler of the Habsburg lands.

### The Czech National Revival

The late 1700s through the 1800s saw the emergence of the Czech National Revival movement. After well over a century of being forced to hide their traditions, the Czech people strove to regain their own culture. One of the first missions of the revival was to bring the Czech language back to life. Although it was still spoken in private, the language had not been taught in schools or used in literature for a long time. Its instruction was reinstated in schools, and in 1834 the first Czech language dictionary was created by Josef Jungmann.

Workers at a factory in northern Bohemia handle a huge sheet of glass. Factories sprang up through the Czech region in the late 1800s and early 1900s.

As the industrial revolution swept across Europe, Czechs built their first major railway in 1845, stretching between Prague and Vienna. Manufacturing regions that had already been established along transportation waterways grew rapidly, using water power to run factories. Politically, 1848 saw the first attempts by Czechs to seriously establish a federalist government. By the end of the century, a Czech national identity had reemerged. Evidence of this can be found in the establishment of the National Theater in 1883 and the National Museum in 1890.

In 1914, the assassination of Archduke Franz Ferdinand, heir to the Austro-Hungarian throne, marked the end of the Habsburg bloodline and served as the spark that started World War I. From 1914 to 1918, the Czech people fought alongside the Germans, Austrians, and Hungarians against Russia and countries in western Europe. They were defeated, and the Habsburgs' Austro-Hungarian Empire fell for good. This left the Czechs, as well as other Habsburg subjects, free to govern themselves.

**The National Theater was built on the banks of the Vltava, facing Prague Castle. It is a monument to the Czechs' belief in the importance of Czech language and culture.**

## A Short-Lived Independence

On October 28, 1918, the independent state of Czechoslovakia was born. The territory included both what are now the Czech Republic and the country of Slovakia. Its capital was established in Prague. Prague Castle became the offices for the newly elected government, and the first president of Czechoslovakia, Tomas Garrigue Masaryk, took office. Under its new parliamentary democracy, Czechoslovakia experienced two decades of unparalleled prosperity. Unfortunately, the young country would not enjoy its freedom from foreign rule for long, and the worst was yet to come.

## World War II

In September 1938, France, Italy, Great Britain, and Germany signed an agreement called the Munich Pact. This agreement gave Adolf Hitler, the leader of Nazi Germany, permission to invade Czechoslovakia without intervention from the other countries, despite the fact that France had agreed to be a defensive ally to the young nation. The phrase "*O nas bez nas*," which means "about us, without us," is a national saying that bitterly refers to that fateful day. The following spring, on

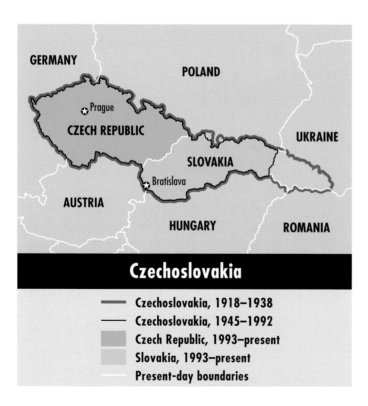

### Czechoslovakia

— Czechoslovakia, 1918–1938
— Czechoslovakia, 1945–1992
 Czech Republic, 1993–present
 Slovakia, 1993–present
— Present-day boundaries

March 15, 1939, German troops crossed the border and began their six-and-a-half-year occupation of Czechoslovakia.

**German troops march into Czechoslovakia in 1939.**

Life immediately changed for every Czech person, and for many it meant imprisonment or death. The Nazis were intensely nationalistic and believed that northern Europeans were racially superior. They hated Jewish people and ethnic and racial minorities. They forced everyone in Czechoslovakia to provide proof of their heritage back three generations. Anyone who could not do this, had Jewish ancestry, or belonged to the Roma ethnic group was shipped to labor camps, concentration camps, or extermination facilities. Anyone opposing the Nazis

## Hidden Factories

During World War II, the forces fighting Germany targeted Nazi military factories where weapons and aircraft were manufactured. From bomber planes above, large factory buildings were easy to see, but an underground factory was completely invisible to aircraft. The Nazis took full advantage of the numerous mining caves and railroad tunnels in the karst-filled Czech territory by establishing their factories beneath the ground.

Using prisoners from concentration camps, existing tunnels were dug deeper and bigger to make room for weapons production and even airplane construction. The Richard Factory near Litomerice was the largest and cost the lives of five thousand prisoners from the camp at Terezin. Today, some of these former underground factories are open to the public as historic sites and memorials to those who lost their lives building them.

was severely punished or executed. Those who remained were forced to work long hours in factories building Hitler's war machines.

In Czechoslovakia, Jews and Roma were the main targets of Nazi persecution. Jewish people were identified by both religion and ancestry and were forced to wear a yellow star to identify themselves. The Nazis confiscated their property and soon began to imprison them. In 1939, at the beginning of the Nazi occupation, nearly 120,000 Jews lived in the area that is now the Czech Republic. By 1945, the end of World War II, fewer than 15,000 survived. Many had been shipped out of the country to death camps such as Auschwitz, in Poland. Others were sent to work camps, where some managed to survive starvation and illness.

Some non-Jewish Czechs had the courage to stand up against the Nazis. In October 1939, a group of students held a demonstration in Prague's Wenceslas Square and Old Town Square, which resulted in the Nazis closing all Czech universities. Citizens of Prague refused to give in completely, however.

## The Terezin Camp

In late 1941, the Nazis opened a concentration camp at Terezin, north of Prague. The Germans called it Theresienstadt. For Czech Jews and Roma, the Terezin camp served as a holding area where they waited to find out if they would be shipped to an extermination camp. Roughly 140,000 people were brought to Terezin, 90,000 of whom were later sent to death camps. Out of the 15,000 children brought to the camp, fewer than 1,100 survived. The living conditions were cramped and filthy, there was little food, and disease ran rampant. Although prisoners were not executed, approximately 33,000 people died of hunger, disease, and maltreatment in the three and a half years the camp was open.

Despite this, the prisoners maintained an astonishing cultural life. Prisoners kept a library and established secret classrooms to teach their children. Artists created paintings and drawings, musicians kept music in the air, writers wove tales, and actors entertained. The Terezin Memorial honors the memory of those who were subjected to the horrors of the Holocaust and racial persecution. It also contains a museum that preserves the artwork, stories, and evidence of what the prisoners endured, reminding visitors of the durability of the human spirit.

By 1944, they were refusing to use German currency. They tore down German street signs, and even took over the radio station by force. This was known as the Prague Uprising, which was the beginning of the end of Nazi occupation. In February 1945, eastern Bohemia and Moravia were liberated by troops from the Soviet Union, and western Bohemia was freed by American troops.

**German bombers destroyed houses in central Prague during the Prague Uprising.**

## A Half-Century of Oppression

At the end of World War II, Edward Benes, who had been the Czech president prior to the German occupation, again became president. In the aftermath of the war, resentment toward Germans and Hungarians was high. Under the so-called Benes decrees, millions of ethnic Germans and Hungarians were stripped of their Czech citizenship. Many were forced to leave the country.

Millions of ethnic Germans lived in Czechoslovakia at the beginning of World War II. At the war's end, many were forced to leave for Germany.

**Communist militia members march through Prague after the nation's anti-communist leaders were forced to resign and the communists took control.**

The Communist Party of Czechoslovakia won the elections in 1946. For a time, communists and non-communists tried to work together, but by early 1948, the communists had taken complete control. The Czechs had traded one oppressor for another. Most private companies were taken over by the government, which controlled the economy. Human rights and political freedoms were eliminated, and those who criticized the regime were harassed by the secret police. The police had the right to search homes at any time, interrogate anyone suspected of associating with someone who opposed the regime, and imprison anyone for any reason at all.

Czechoslovakia fell under the control of the Soviet Union. Czech officials were ordered by the Soviet leader Joseph Stalin to conduct "purges" in the 1950s. Political and military leaders were targeted, arrested, and put on public trial. These were known as "show trials," and the entire process was staged. The accused were forced to rehearse pre-written testimony, and the outcome was always a guilty verdict with a sentence of execution. Nearly two hundred people were killed during this time for standing up to the totalitarian regime.

In the 1960s, Czech political leader Alexander Dubcek tried to ease the harsher aspects of communism. Government policy changed to allow greater personal freedom and democracy. This movement became known as the Prague Spring.

**A Czechoslovak banknote from 1960 shows girls picking flowers. Many bills from Czechoslovakia's communist era depict romanticized scenes of farmers and workers.**

Angry with these changes, the Soviets invaded Czechoslovakia on August 21, 1968, and took control of the government. This marked the beginning of two more years of purges, punishing anyone involved in the reform efforts. Literature and entertainment were censored, and rock music

**Students demonstrate in favor of more freedom during the Prague Spring protests of 1968.**

fans were even punished for listening to Western music. Schools discouraged free thought and were only allowed to teach limited subjects. The communists were again in firm control.

**The Soviet Union sent tanks into Prague to end the Prague Spring. Czechs watch as a tank crashes into a building.**

## The Velvet Revolution

By the 1980s, neighboring countries such as Poland, Hungary, and East Germany were trying to escape totalitarian rule. Demand for change was happening across Eastern Europe. By November 1989, huge protests were being held in cities across Czechoslovakia. People were demanding an end to one-party rule. By the end of November, the country's communist leaders had resigned, and on December 29, the nation

## Playwright and Politician

Vaclav Havel was a playwright, activist, and politician who spent his life fighting for Czech freedom and progress. When he was born in 1936, his family was already well established as politically active intellectuals. Throughout his childhood, they continued to speak out against both the Nazi and communist regimes. As a result of the political activity, the government would not allow Havel to attend a college with a humanities program, in an effort to discourage him from following in his parents' footsteps.

As a young man, Havel studied drama while working as a stage technician, and he soon began writing

his own plays. His writing expanded to essays and poetry, and eventually to speeches and letters, which brought him into the political spotlight.

He became an important figure in the Prague Spring of 1968. In the following decades, the communists sent him to prison many times because he spoke out against their oppression. He eventually organized the Civic Forum, a political group that worked to overthrow the communist regime. In 1989, following the Velvet Revolution, he was elected president of Czechoslovakia. Then, in 1993, he was elected the first president of the new nation of the Czech Republic. He served as president for another ten years, during which he was instrumental in the nation becoming part of NATO, the North Atlantic Treaty Organization. After his presidency, he remained politically active as a writer. Havel died in 2011 and was mourned worldwide.

swore in its new president, Vaclav Havel, an outspoken critic of communism who had been imprisoned many times for speaking out publicly. This peaceful change in government is known as the Velvet Revolution.

## Recent Times

Without communist control, tensions between the Czech and Slovak parts of the country rose to the surface. The Czech region was wealthier, and the Slovaks wanted greater political

**Hundreds of thousands of people attend a rally in Prague in November 1989 to demand an end to communism in Czechoslovakia.**

control of their region. Although less than 40 percent of the people in either region wanted the nation to dissolve, it quietly broke apart at the end of 1992. On January 1, 1993, the new nation of the Czech Republic was born.

In the years that followed, the Czech Republic went through the difficult process of converting its economy to

A border guard takes down a Czechoslovakian border sign on January 1, 1993, the day the Czech Republic and Slovakia separated.

capitalism. Companies that had been run by the government were returned to private hands. Gradually, the economy improved.

In 2004, the Czech Republic became a member of the European Union (EU), a political and economic union of most of the nations in Europe. Goods and people are allowed to move freely between member nations of the EU. Nineteen EU nations use a common currency called the euro, but the Czech Republic continues to use its traditional currency, the Czech koruna. Membership in the EU has helped the Czech economy continue to improve. In recent years, it has had one of the strongest economies in formerly communist Europe. Despite their long history of oppression, the Czechs have emerged from their trials stronger than before.

Today, Prague is a thriving city with its own unique sense of humor. In 2010, sculptures of crawling babies were added to a concrete TV tower from the 1960s, which had frequently been called the ugliest building in the world.

# CHAPTER 5

# Independence and Democracy

**T**HE CZECH REPUBLIC IS A PARLIAMENTARY REPUBLIC. The government is divided into three branches: executive, legislative, and judicial. This structure was established by the adoption of the Czech Constitution on December 16, 1992. It became effective January 1, 1993, the date that the Czech Republic and Slovakia became independent nations. This is known as the Restoration Day of the Independent Czech State.

*Opposite:* **Wallenstein Palace was built in the 1600s as the home of a prominent duke. Today, it houses the Czech Senate.**

## Executive Branch

The executive branch of government is in charge of running the government and ensuring that the laws are carried out. In the Czech Republic, the leader of the executive branch is the president. According to the Czech constitution that went into effect in 1993, members of Parliament select the president.

## Celebrating Independence Day, but Which One?

The Czech Republic came into existence when Czechoslovakia split apart into the Czech Republic and Slovakia in January 1993. But in the century before that, the Czech people gained independence from outside rule three times. In 1989 came the end of Soviet communist domination. In 1945, the Soviets liberated the Czechs from six horrifying years of Nazi tyranny. Looking back even further, the Republic of Czechoslovakia became independent from the Austro-Hungarian Empire in 1918, following World War I. October 28, the day Czechoslovakia became independent, is the official Independence Day of the Czech Republic.

Czechs became dissatisfied with their lack of voice, however, and the constitution was changed. Since 2013, the president has been directly elected by voters. If no candidate receives more than 50 percent of the votes in a presidential election, a second election is held between the two highest vote-getters. A president can serve no more than two consecutive five-year terms. Among the president's most important duties is appointing high government officials, including the head of government, called the prime minister.

The prime minister is responsible for the direct administration of government. He or she chooses cabinet officers, who must be approved by the president. The cabinet is made up of officials who are in charge of various parts of the government.

## National Government of the Czech Republic

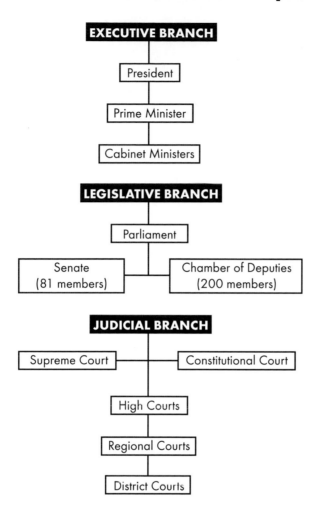

**EXECUTIVE BRANCH**

President

Prime Minister

Cabinet Ministers

**LEGISLATIVE BRANCH**

Parliament

Senate
(81 members)

Chamber of Deputies
(200 members)

**JUDICIAL BRANCH**

Supreme Court

Constitutional Court

High Courts

Regional Courts

District Courts

These include the minister of defense, the minister of agriculture, and the minister of culture. The prime minister is also responsible for designing and implementing policies, with the help of the cabinet. The prime minister's efforts are supported by the deputy prime minister.

**Milos Zeman, the president of the Czech Republic, speaks during a session of the Chamber of Deputies.**

## Legislative Branch

The legislative branch of government is responsible for making and reviewing all laws. In the Czech Republic, this is called the Parliament. It is made up of two houses, the Senate and the Chamber of Deputies.

The Senate has eighty-one members, directly elected by citizens. If no candidate receives a majority of the total votes cast, a runoff election is held to determine a winner. Members serve six-year terms, with one-third of the seats subject to election every two years.

The Chamber of Deputies has two hundred members who are elected by voters to represent specific regions, so areas with higher populations will vote for more representatives than areas that have smaller populations. Members of the Chamber of Deputies serve four-year terms.

### Heart of the Nation

Prague is the center of the executive and legislative branches of the Czech government. In 2017, Prague had an estimated population of 1,165,581, while the population of the metropolitan area was estimated to be more than 2,300,000 people.

Prague is the fifth most visited city in Europe, renowned for its history, architecture, museums, theaters, and active cultural life. It is also a bustling economic city, home to many technology, engineering, and pharmaceutical companies. The service industry has grown during the past several decades, and it now dominates the economy, employing 80 percent

of the workforce. Financial institutions and government account for much of this, and services such as hotels, restaurants, and transportation are another large sector. About half of the nation's tourism revenue comes from visitors to the capital city.

One of the most popular sites to visit is Prague Castle, which dates back to 880. According to legend, it was built because of a vision by a Slavic princess named Libuse, wife of a Premysl prince. The sprawling site is the world's largest castle complex. It served first as the seat of the Premyslid dynasty and hosted many ruling families over the centuries. Today, it serves as the home to the president of the Czech Republic and the headquarters of government offices.

The winding streets and alleys of Prague's Old Town, which was established as early as 1234, also attract throngs of visitors. The Old Town Square is the heart of the city's historic district. It is the site of the Old Town Hall Tower, which features an astronomical clock with figures that move when each hour strikes. Prague is also home to one of the oldest universities in Europe, Charles University, established in 1348.

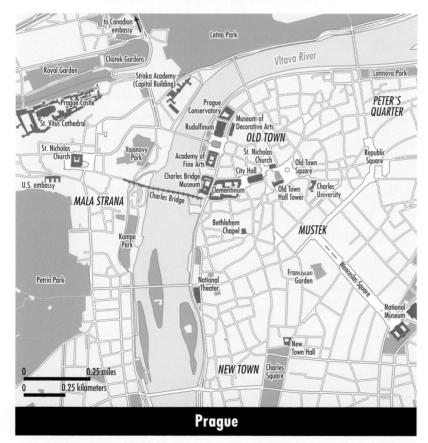

Prague

Judges attend a conference in Brno. Czech trials do not have juries. Instead, one or more judges determine the outcome.

## Judicial Branch

The judicial branch of government consists of the court system. The nation's top courts are all based in Brno. The highest court of appeal in the Czech Republic is the Supreme Court, which is divided into a Civil Law Division, a Commercial Division, and a Criminal Law Division. Each of these has a chief justice, a vice justice, and several associate judges. The Supreme Court judges review decisions made in lower courts.

The court system also has a Constitutional Court, which is made up of fifteen judges. This court rules on issues such as whether laws violate the constitution. The Supreme Administrative Court, which has twenty-eight judges, deals with administrative issues and questions such as whether individuals are eligible to run for office.

Candidates for Supreme Court judgeships are proposed by the Chamber of Deputies and appointed by the president. They are lifetime appointments. Candidates for Constitutional

Court judgeships are appointed by the president and confirmed by the Senate for ten-year terms. Supreme Administrative Court judges are selected by the president for unlimited terms.

Lower courts are involved with day-to-day hearings and trials for criminal and civil issues. These courts are located throughout the regions and municipalities of the Czech Republic and include high courts, regional courts, and district courts.

Since the end of communism in what is now the Czech Republic and the installation of a democratic government, Parliament and the Czech courts have spent considerable effort revising the nation's legal code to better reflect the current governmental system. A complete revision of the criminal laws was completed in 2010. It modernized the laws and brought Czech criminal law into line with other European democracies. A new civil code was adopted in 2014 that more clearly defined noncriminal laws and made them consistent with civil law in the rest of Europe.

## National Flag

The flag of the Czech Republic features a horizontal white stripe on the top and a horizontal red stripe on the bottom. A blue triangle cuts into these stripes from the left. The flag dates back to 1920, when the blue triangle was added to the two-stripe white and red flag of Bohemia, to create the Czech flag. It was the national flag of the former Czechoslovakia from 1920 to 1993. When the Czech Republic and Slovakia split apart, Slovakia adopted a new flag while the Czech Republic retained the existing design.

## The Military

The Czech government is actively involved in both European and world politics. A major step for the nation's national security was joining the North Atlantic Treaty Organization (NATO) in 1999. NATO is a military alliance among the United States, Canada, and many European nations. With this membership comes both protection and responsibility because an attack against one NATO member is considered an attack against them all.

The Czech military is divided into two branches, the Land Forces and the Air Forces. Czech men and women between the ages of eighteen and twenty-eight can join the military, but it is required that they give up any membership in a political party.

**Czech ground forces take part in training in western Bohemia.**

## National Anthem

The Czech national anthem, "*Kde domov muj?*" ("Where Is My Home?"), was written in 1834, with words by Josef Kajetan Tyl and music by Frantisek Skroup. It was originally a song for a musical play. The song gained popularity and became the first part of the national anthem for the Republic of Czechoslovakia when the nation became independent in 1918. The second part was a Slovak song. When the Czech Republic separated from Slovakia in 1993, the Czech part became the Czech national anthem.

| Czech lyrics | English translation |
| --- | --- |
| *Kde domov muj, kde domov muj,* | Where is my home, where is my home? |
| *Voda huci po lucinach,* | Water roars over the grasslands, |
| *bory sumí po skalinach,* | pines whisper over the mountains, |
| *v sade skvi se jara kvet,* | a spring flower blooms in the orchard, |
| *zemsky raj to na pohled!* | a paradise on Earth, as you can see! |
| *A to je ta krasna zeme,* | And it is that beautiful land, |
| *zeme ceska domov muj,* | Czech land, my home, |
| *zeme ceska domov muj!* | Czech land, my home! |

# CHAPTER 6

# Tradition and Enterprise

**S**ERVICES AND MANUFACTURING ARE THE DRIVING forces in the economy of the Czech Republic. About 38 percent of the workforce is employed in manufacturing, and about 60 percent work in the service sector. Natural resources have been helpful in providing raw materials to manufacturing companies, and historically the country's central location along European trade routes has made trade easy. Since the Czech Republic joined the EU in 2004, trade with other EU nations has become even simpler, helping boost the nation's economy.

*Opposite:* **Workers paint a building in Prague.**

## Natural Resources

The Czech Republic's primary resources are located in small concentrated areas. In the northwest are large deposits of brown coal, also known as lignite. This is a lower quality coal because it burns at a lower temperature and also creates more pollution than higher grade coals.

**Resources**

| | | |
|---|---|---|
| Pasture | C Coal | Pb Lead |
| Grains, sugar beets | Cu Copper | Sn Tin |
| Grains, rapeseed, potatoes | Fe Iron | U Uranium |
| Orchards, vineyards | K Kaolin | W Tungsten |
| Forest | Oil | Zn Zinc |

The higher grade hard coal, often called black coal, is found in generous seams in the southwest in the Pilsen and Central Bohemian regions and throughout the Moravian-Silesian region surrounding the city of Ostrava. These areas have many coal-burning power plants, and a good portion of the country's power comes from these areas.

Iron ore is also found in areas that are rich in high-quality coal, as well as in central Bohemia southwest of Prague. Iron and steel processing plants are located in larger mining areas.

The Karlovy Vary area of western Bohemia contains deposits of uranium. During the communist era, the area's uranium was mined extensively, providing the Soviet Union with a generous supply of the radioactive elements, which are used in many nuclear weapons and in nuclear power plants. Currently, the mine at the small town of Rozna is the only operating uranium mine in Europe. The uranium is both exported and used domestically as a source for nuclear power.

Czech forests have also been harvested for centuries. As a result, very little of the original forest growth remains. The forests provided fuel for furnaces, timber for homes, and pulp to make paper. The wood was also used in artistic ways. In southern Bohemia and central Moravia, the art of furniture making became an important industry. Wooden musical instruments also became a specialty, and the ones from this nation continue to be some of the best in the world.

## Industrial Evolution

Early industry began with trade routes along the main rivers, especially the Elbe into Germany, and to the south from Moravia along rivers like the Oder. During the 1500s, handspun and handwoven textiles were commonly made by

**Workers travel through a coal mine in the Czech Republic. The nation consumes almost all of the coal it produces.**

## Czech Currency

The Czech Republic's official currency is the koruna. A koruna is divided into one hundred hellers. Heller coins were taken out of circulation in 2003, but merchants still use the heller in pricing. The total price of the items is then rounded up or down to the nearest koruna.

The smallest denomination available is the 1-koruna coin. Coins also come in values of 2, 5, 10, 20, and 50 korunas. Czech banknotes, or paper currency, come in denominations of 100, 200, 500, 1,000, 2,000, and 5,000 korunas. Each denomination has a different color scheme and depicts an important figure from Czech history on the front. The 100-koruna note, for example, is pink and green and bears a portrait of the Father of the Country, Charles IV. Other Czech men and women honored on banknotes include philosopher John Amos Comenius, opera singer Ema Destinnova, and writer Bozena Nemcova. In 2017, 1 koruna equaled US$0.05, and 22 korunas equaled US$1.00.

individuals in their homes and then bought and transported to a warehouse to be sold.

By the early 1700s, glassmaking had become a profitable business for the regions below the Sumava and Jizera Mountains. These areas were rich in siliceous sand required to make glass, and just as importantly, full of forests that provided the heat and charcoal necessary to produce it. Czech crystal was highly desired, not only for its high quality but also for its price, which was much lower than the famed glass from Venice, Italy.

The eighteenth century also saw the beginnings of the

paper industry, and the sugar industry using sugar beets. Porcelain and ceramic production began to flourish in western Bohemia, especially the Karlovy Vary region where the necessary minerals are plentiful. As technology advanced, early factories were built, usually along rivers, to power machinery.

As the industrial revolution spread through Europe, Czech factories grew and expanded. In 1894, the Bata shoe company was founded. It quickly made a name for itself internationally. During the first twenty years after the formation of Czechoslovakia, the country was a world leader in glass, textiles, and shoes. Textiles remained a major industry in the

**Workers inspect newly made boots at a Bata factory in the Czech Republic.**

region until the 1990s, when the Czechs could no longer compete with the cheap and plentiful Chinese products.

When communism came with the promise of a centralized, stable economy and equality, people were hopeful that they would thrive again. Instead, individual businesses and farms were forced to become part of collectives, and the government controlled every aspect of industry. Again, the natural resources of the country were exploited as its leaders focused on manufacturing machinery and heavy equipment and exporting coal. With the fall of communism, the economy suffered while industry adjusted to the political changes.

## What the Czech Republic Grows, Makes, and Mines

**AGRICULTURE**

| | |
|---|---|
| Wheat (2015) | 5,274,272 metric tons |
| Sugar beets (2015) | 3,421,025 metric tons |
| Pigs (2016) | 1,609,945 animals |

**MANUFACTURING (VALUE ADDED, 2014)**

| | |
|---|---|
| Transportation equipment | $9,700,000,000 |
| Metal products | $5,300,000,000 |
| Machinery | $4,800,000,000 |

**MINING**

| | |
|---|---|
| Lignite (2016) | 38,400,000 metric tons |
| Hard coal (2016) | 8,400,000 metric tons |
| Kaolin clay (2013) | 3,108,000 metric tons |

## Skoda Auto

The automobile industry is a source of Czech pride thanks to the Skoda Auto company. Founded in 1895, it is one of the oldest car manufacturing companies in the world. It began by manufacturing motorcycles and within ten years was producing a limousine. The company excelled until World War II, but once Czechoslovakia became communist, the government directed how it was run. As communism was declining, Skoda Auto became a Volkswagen brand and secured its place as a respected European auto manufacturer.

In addition to cars, the company designs and makes a wide range of products, including the Skoda-Inekon 10T, a tram car used all over the world. It is also known for engineering and manufacturing industrial drills, lathes, and other tools as well as power-generating equipment like steam turbines.

## Modern Industry

The Czech Republic's modern economy has come a long way in its recovery. Abandoned factory towns are beginning to revive with new industries, such as power generation, after the more recent decline in textiles and other goods. Longstanding industries like glass, coal, steel, and heavy machinery are still going strong, while newer pursuits such as electronics, technology, chemicals, and medicines have been growing.

Automotive equipment is now the country's largest manufacturing industry. In 2016, machinery and transportation equipment accounted for 56.3 percent of the country's total exports. The ERA company in Pardubice is a leading producer of military equipment, and the Czech Ministry of Defense

## Unique Czech Products

*Bata Footwear Company:* Founded in 1894 by Tomas Bata in the city of Zlin, in Moravia, this company revolutionized the shoe industry by using textiles to make footwear rather than using the more expensive leather. Because the company's shoes were more affordable than other shoes, Bata grew rapidly. The company's growth helped Zlin expand with its own housing complex, schools, and recreational areas. Unlike many businesses, Bata grew during World War II because of the new demand for military footwear. Today, the company employs more than fifty thousand people in its factories and retail stores worldwide.

*Petrof Pianos:* Antonin Petrof began crafting pianos in 1864, and five generations later, his family still operates the factory based in Hradec Kralove, a city in northeastern Bohemia. The company specializes in grand pianos, which can be found in some of the greatest opera houses around the world.

*GZ Media Records:* Decades after CDs nearly ended the vinyl record industry, records have once again become popular, and a company in Lodenice has become the world's leading manufacturer of them. In 2011, GZ Media signed exclusive contracts with the world's top music production companies, including Universal and Sony. Since then, production has soared, and in 2016 the company produced almost twenty-four million records.

*Pilsner Urquell Brewing Company (left):* Pilsner Urquell got its start in 1842 when founder Josef Groll brewed the first batch of a new type of beer, later named Pilsner. It is distinct because of its pale color and mild flavor. The company now markets many varieties and its beverages are sold internationally.

*GUFEX Pucks (above):* The northern Moravian company GUFEX is a rubber manufacturer that specializes in hockey pucks. Their pucks have been used in the Olympics, and they have an exclusive contract with the International Ice Hockey Federation. They export 90 percent of their pucks, half of which are sold in the United States.

oversees the company that makes the Sojka drone, an airplane that allows surveillance without risking the pilot's life.

**Czech workers harvest kohlrabi, a vegetable that is similar to a turnip but is related to broccoli.**

## Agriculture

Agriculture makes up only about 3 percent of the Czech economy and employs less than 3 percent of the workforce. Important products include sugar beets, and grains such as wheat, barley, and rye. Hops, an important ingredient in beer, are also grown in the Czech Republic.

Some Czech farmers raise livestock such as dairy cows, beef cows, and pigs. Chickens are also commonly raised.

### Services

The service sector is the largest part of the Czech economy. Especially in Prague, many people work in banking, finance, and government positions. Other service jobs include health care, information technology, and advertising.

Another major part of the service sector of the economy is the tourism industry. Many Czechs work in hotels, restaurants, spas, and parks, all of which serve visitors. People working in transportation and sales also benefit from the nation's recent growth in tourism. In 2015, the country hosted nearly twenty-eight million foreign visitors.

**Czechs and tourists enjoy relaxing in the nation's cafés.**

## The European Union

In 2004, the Czech Republic became a member of the European Union (EU). This has brought both promise and apprehension. Benefits of EU membership include removing all trade and employment restrictions with other EU countries, allowing Czechs to be part of a bigger, more diverse economic system. EU countries are also eligible to receive funding to help with improvements, such as finding new industries for the former textile regions. Many Czechs feel that EU membership has given the country much-needed support.

Despite these benefits, some people worry about membership. Some people remember the past struggles of their small country when it was swallowed by the economic agendas of foreign powers, while others worry that Czech traditions might be lost.

Czechs fill a streetcar in Prague. People take more than three hundred million rides on the city's streetcars every year.

# CHAPTER 7

# The Czech People

THE CZECH REPUBLIC'S CENTRAL LOCATION AND history have given it a diverse ethnic identity that is a mix of both eastern and western European culture. Those who identify as part of the Czech ethnic group may base it on family heritage, cultural upbringing, or both. The majority of these are descendants of early west Slavic migrants. These early settlers, often referred to as Bohemians, mixed with the existing Germanic and Celtic tribes, creating a unique ethnic identity.

Czech cultural heritage has been threatened many times by the groups that ruled the region, from the Hungarian Premyslid dynasty to Austrian Habsburgs in the distant past to the Nazi and Soviet powers in more recent times. Each has attempted to repress and replace the Czech culture, yet it has held strong and endured. One major effort to keep Czech

*Opposite:* **Children chase bubbles on a damp day in Prague.**

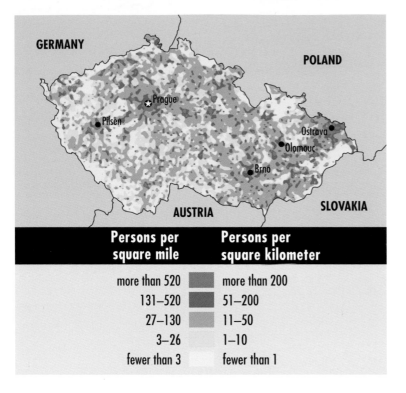

| Persons per square mile | | Persons per square kilometer |
|---|---|---|
| more than 520 | | more than 200 |
| 131–520 | | 51–200 |
| 27–130 | | 11–50 |
| 3–26 | | 1–10 |
| fewer than 3 | | fewer than 1 |

**Population of Major Cities (2017 est.)**

| | |
|---|---|
| Prague | 1,165,581 |
| Brno | 369,559 |
| Ostrava | 313,088 |
| Pilsen | 164,180 |
| Olomouc | 101,268 |

**Ethnic Groups**

| | |
|---|---|
| Czech | 64% |
| Moravian | 5% |
| Slovak | 1.4% |
| Not identified | 25% |
| Other | 4% |

ethnic identity strong was the Czech National Revival, which began in the late 1700s after generations were forced to hide their traditions.

## By the Numbers

At the end of 2016, the population of the Czech Republic was 10,578,820. The country is home to about 500,000 foreign residents, half of whom are permanent residents. About three-quarters of the population lives in cities or city suburbs.

In addition to the Czechs, other ethnic groups found in the country include Moravians, Slovaks, and small populations of Ukrainians, Poles, Germans, and Hungarians. A full quarter of the people in the last official census did not choose any ethnic heritage at all.

In the 2011 census, 64 percent of the nation's residents identified Czech as at least one of their primary ethnicities. They could also choose a second. Just a decade earlier, in the 2001 census where only one ethnicity could be picked, 89 percent identified themselves as primarily Czech. Czech membership in the EU may be a factor in this shift, since citizens of one EU country may now move to another, searching for different job opportunities across Europe.

### The Czech Language

More than 95 percent of all residents of the Czech Republic speak Czech as their first language. Czech evolved from ancient Slavic languages, which are also the basis of other eastern European tongues such as Polish and Russian. During the 1600s, German rulers attempted to eradicate the language as part of their suppression of Czech culture, but they were unsuccessful.

**More than eighty thousand people of Vietnamese descent live in the Czech Republic. Most live in Prague or in the Karlovy Vary region near the German border.**

## A People at Risk

One of the Czech Republic's smallest ethnic groups is the Roma. The ancestors of the Roma people arrived in Europe perhaps a thousand years ago from India. Today, they live across Europe and in many other parts of the world. Historically, they have led transient lifestyles and have been treated as outcasts. During World War II, the Nazis persecuted the Roma. Only about 10 percent of the Czech Roma population survived World War II. In the 2011 census, more than thirteen thousand people indicated Roma as one of their two primary ethnicities.

The Roma people have long been discriminated against in the Czech Republic and elsewhere. Because of the long history of discrimination and oppression, it is difficult for Roma people to escape poverty. Many employers refuse to hire Roma workers, and Roma children do not always have the same educational opportunities as other Czech students. Membership in the EU has given some Roma hope of finding greater opportunities, because the EU has laws protecting the rights of ethnic minorities.

The Museum of Romani Culture in Brno was established in 1991 to document and celebrate all aspects of Roma culture and history. Exhibits include dwellings, clothing, and art, telling the story of the Roma people from their beginnings through today. The museum has also committed to helping tutor disadvantaged children, especially Roma students.

As in many countries, people who live in different regions of the Czech Republic speak with varying dialects, or versions of the language. With Czech, however, people who speak different dialects can understand each other. Written Czech and spoken Czech are very different, not in vocabulary but in pronunciations and in the endings of words.

The Czech language uses many accents and other marks to indicate how a certain letter or group of letters should be pronounced. In addition to the twenty-six letters used in the English alphabet, the Czech language includes the letters *á, č, ď, é, ě, í, ň, ó, ř, š, ť, ú, ů, ý,* and *ž.* For example, *á, é, í, ú, ů,* and

**A woman watches the street below from her home in Slavonice, in southern Moravia. Moravia has more dialects than Bohemia.**

## The Father of Modern Czech

Josef Jungmann (1773–1847) was born in the village of Hudlice to a Czech mother and German Bohemian father. Both Czech and German were spoken in his household, and he grew up fluent in both languages. After finishing school, he went on to become a teacher at a high school in Litomerice and then later a professor at Prague's Charles University. During his time at the university, Jungmann began to translate the works of classic authors into the Czech language.

Eventually, Jungmann began to write original texts, starting with the textbook *Slovesnost* in 1820. Five years later, he published the *History of Czech Literature*, and over the next decade he wrote the first Czech-German dictionary. It was published in five volumes between 1834 and 1839 and marked a major step in the Czech National Revival. In an attempt to legitimize the Czech language as having a vocabulary worthy of complex literature, he revived old words and expanded the vocabulary with additional Slavic words. He is credited with being the founder of the modern Czech language.

ý are long vowels. Ú and ů are pronounced the same, but ú is usually found at the beginning of a word, while ů is only found in the middle or end.

Ě is a "softening" vowel that is used only in conjunction with consonants. For example, *bě* is pronounced like "bje" and *mě* is pronounced like "mně."

## How Do You Say . . . ?

| Hello | Dobry den |
| Good-bye | Na shledanou |
| What's your name? | Jak se jmenujete? |
| My name is . . . | Jmenuji se  . . . |
| How are you? | Jak se mate? |
| I'm fine, thank you. | Mam se dobre, dekuji. |
| Do you speak English? | Mluvite anglicky? |
| I don't speak Czech. | Nemluvim cesky. |
| What time is it? | Kolik je hodin? |
| It was nice meeting you. | Rad jsem vas poznal. |

**A street sign for Old Town Square in Prague**

# CHAPTER 8

# Spiritual Traditions

THROUGHOUT MUCH OF CZECH HISTORY, RELIGION played a major part in the government. During the days of the Holy Roman Empire, church and state were fully combined, and religious law was treated the same as any other law. In 1415, Jan Hus, a critic of the church's abuse of power, was burned at the stake for the crime of heresy. This began the Hussite Revolution, the country's first large-scale religious conflict. It was the first of many conflicts between Catholics and Protestants.

Already a minority that had been subjected to centuries of oppression, Jewish people became the focus of religious hatred during World War II. Christianity became mandatory under Nazi rule. When communists took over following the war, atheism—no belief in God—became the official policy of Czechoslovakia. The churches were taken over by the government. The Czechs did not regain full religious freedom until 1989. Since then, organized religion has not been widely practiced by the Czechs.

*Opposite:* **Catholic priests take part in a procession in Stara Boleslav, in central Bohemia. Many Catholics make pilgrimages to the city, the site of St. Wenceslas's death.**

A baroque church in Prague

## Religion in the Czech Republic (2011)

| | |
|---|---|
| Roman Catholic Church | 10.3% |
| Evangelical Church of Czech Brethren | 0.5% |
| Czechoslovak Hussite Church | 0.4% |
| Jehovah's Witnesses | 0.1% |
| Judaism | 0.01% |
| Unspecified religion | 8.5% |
| No response | 44.7% |
| No religion | 34.5% |

### Religion Today

Thirty religions are recognized in the Czech Republic today. Nearly 35 percent of the population say they have no religion. And a little over 10 percent identify as Roman Catholic. Protestants make up about 1 percent, and other religions such as Judaism and Islam are represented in small numbers. Nearly 45 percent of those surveyed in the 2011 census did not give a response concerning religion.

### Holidays

Despite the relatively low number of people in the Czech Republic who are actively religious, the major Christian holidays of Christmas and Easter are celebrated with enthusiasm.

Christmas is a time when families gather to celebrate together, and many old Czech traditions are followed during the holiday season. Christmas trees and festive decorations fill homes and public spaces, and Christmas markets are an event that everyone looks forward to each year.

The Easter holiday is also celebrated widely by Czechs as a welcoming of spring. Elaborately decorated Easter eggs called *kraslice* are a popular tradition. They are often crafted by hand and given as gifts.

**Cities and towns across the Czech Republic hold Christmas markets, where food and gifts are sold.**

## Christmas Traditions

The Czechs have a number of Christmas customs and superstitions, many related to health, fortune, and good tidings in the coming year. Few people still believe in them, but some still observe parts of them to keep old traditions alive.

- If people refrain from eating meat all day on Christmas Eve, it is said they will see a golden pig flying through the sky that evening.
- Fried carp is served for Christmas Eve dinner. It is said that if the person preparing the dinner dries a fish scale and puts it in their wallet, it will bring good fortune in the new year.
- The dinner table must be set with an even number of place settings, so an empty one is added if there is an odd number of guests. An odd number of settings is bad luck. Likewise, if anyone sits with their back to the door during the meal, it will bring bad luck upon the family.

- Each person at Christmas dinner cuts an apple in half after the meal. The shape of the pattern in the center indicates the future. If it is star-shaped, it means good fortune. If it comes to four points, it means illness or death.
- If a person gets up from the Christmas dinner table before everyone has finished, it will bring illness and bad luck to the entire family in the coming year.
- Eating garlic or decorating the table with it during the Christmas meal will bring luck and protection in the coming year.

## Kraslice

For the Czech, the Easter tradition of painted eggs goes far beyond food dye and stickers. Using both traditional methods and new materials, experienced decorators spend hours perfecting intricate designs on the shells of hollowed eggs. One technique uses melted beeswax to draw patterns on the egg. The egg is then dyed, which leaves the waxed sections uncolored. Each year there are contests in cities and towns for the most impressive designs.

## Fairy Tales & Myths

Czech culture is full of fairy tales, traditional myths, and superstitions involving luck, marriage, health, and abundance. The stories describe mischievous and often harmful supernatural beings. Most hint at being cautionary tales to keep children (and adults) from danger.

The *vodnik* or *hastrman* is a water sprite that tries to lure children into the water with shiny objects so he can drown them and steal their souls. He is traditionally depicted as green with huge eyes, riding a fish like a horse. The creature stores the souls in a jar beneath the water, and if one manages to escape, it rises to the surface as nothing more than a bubble.

Less frightening spirits found in nature are the will-o'-the-wisps. Legend says they are the souls of dead witches. They are found in the woods and appear as small, moving lights. Some are said to lure travelers off the path, while others help lost travelers find their way. Another forest ghost is the *hejkal*, a loud creature that yells and harasses those who meet it.

**A Czech girl looks at a statue of a vodnik. In some stories, vodniks are strange rather than frightening.**

In Czech legend, ghosts aren't found only in nature. For example, a castle-haunting ghost is called a White Lady. Such ghosts are believed to be the spirits of women, dressed all in white, and their appearance means that danger is near.

Witches and devils are very much a part of Czech mythology. The "midday witch" will steal away misbehaving children at noon, while the "twilight witch" kidnaps children who are out past curfew. Devils are hairy, hooved creatures with horns who seek out desperate people to bargain with in order to get their souls. In return for granting the person's wish, the devil claims the person's soul at death and adds it to a collection of stolen souls.

## The Golem

Many people trace the story of the Golem to a sixteenth-century Prague rabbi named Judah Loew. At the time, the Jewish population of Prague was subjected to violence on a regular basis. The legend says that in an attempt to protect his people, the rabbi created the Golem. He is said to have gathered clay from the banks of the Vltava River and formed the creature. He then brought it to life with a Hebrew incantation and by writing the word *emet* (truth) on its forehead.

According to the story, the Golem at first did exactly as the rabbi asked, and acted as a protector to his people. But the Golem soon took on a life of its own, growing in size and attacking people unprovoked. The rabbi finally agreed to destroy it after being promised that no more harm would come to his community. He removed the first letter from the word on the Golem's forehead, leaving the word *met*, which means "death."

Rabbi Loew died in 1609 and was buried in the Old Jewish Cemetery in Prague (above). It is one of the largest Jewish cemeteries in Europe.

# CHAPTER 9

# Art and Culture

**T**HROUGHOUT THE CENTURIES, CZECH CULTURE HAS endured, despite the many attempts to suppress and erase it. The arts have played an important role in preserving Czech culture, and have provided an outlet for social and political expression. Music has also been an integral part of Czech society, from folk songs to classical music and contemporary rock. Sports are another cultural element that the Czechs take great pride in, both at home and in international competitions.

### Literature and Censorship

Both the Nazi and the communist regimes routinely banned books, plays, and any creative or literary works that were seen as a criticism of their policies. Many Czech writers and playwrights carefully crafted their work so that Czech audiences recognized their allusions to communist oppression, but it was less obvious to officials.

*Opposite:* **A man leaps high into the air while performing a traditional Czech dance.**

### The First Robot

Artist and writer Karel Capek and his brother, Josef, are credited with being the first people to use the word *robot* in its modern context. They came up with it while Karel was looking for a name for the mechanical creatures featured in his play, later named *R.U.R.* (*Rossum's Universal Robots*). The word *robot* was derived from the Czech word *robota*, which means "serf labor" or "slave work" and is used commonly to describe difficult and monotonous work.

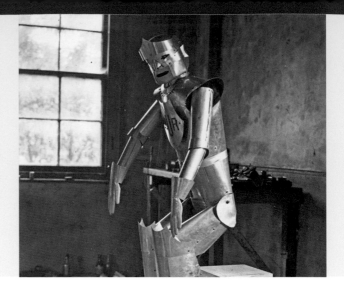

Vaclav Havel's plays were especially successful in disguising rebellious ideas within comedy. *The Memorandum*, for example, parodied the overbearing bureaucracy that Czechs lived under during communist rule. In this play, a fake lan-

**Ludvik Vaculik's writing is known for its humor and humanity.**

### Franz Kafka

Kafka was born in Prague in 1883 to a German-speaking Jewish family. Although he studied to be a lawyer, he earned his living unhappily as an insurance investigator, while writing in his spare time. It is estimated that Kafka burned around 90 percent of his writing. His works that were published did not bring him fame during his lifetime.

His writing is known for absurd premises, depictions of isolation and anxiety, and criticism of capitalism and bureaucracy. In one of his greatest novels, *The Trial*, a man is arrested but never told what his crime is. In 1912, Kafka wrote *The Metamorphosis*, which is about a salesman who finds himself transformed into a huge insect. After Kafka's death in 1924, *The Metamorphosis* became one of the most celebrated works of its time.

guage is introduced into a large organization. It is supposed to make the organization more efficient, but instead causes a complete breakdown of communication. Other politically charged writing included Ludvik Vaculik's 1968 essay "Two Thousand Words," which encouraged people to become active in opposing communism. Vaculik later became one of the authors of Charter 77, a declaration of human rights that was instrumental in the Velvet Revolution.

In the later twentieth century, more experimental writers such as Bohumil Hrabal and Milan Kundera gained prominence. In 1984, poet Jaroslav Seifert became the first Czech to win the Nobel Prize for Literature, the world's highest honor for writers.

## Art and Architecture

The Czech Republic has a strong artistic history. The nation's architecture draws visitors from around the world. There are magnificent examples of gothic architecture. One of the greatest examples is St. Barbara's Church in Kutna Hora, which features three soaring tentlike peaks on top. The country is filled with fantastic baroque architecture, which is noted for its dramatic and exuberant decoration, such as in St. Nicholas Church in Prague.

In the late nineteenth century, a style of art called art

**Alphonse Mucha was renowned for his flowing figures.**

nouveau became popular. It used elegant, curved shapes and designs inspired by plants and flowers. Czech painter Alphonse Mucha gained worldwide fame for his art nouveau posters and paintings. He gained an international following, had a studio in Paris, and taught in the United States, but his heart was in his Czech homeland. For nearly twenty years, he worked on an epic group of monumental paintings inspired by Czech history and mythology. In 1928, his *Slav Epic* was unveiled as a gift to the people of Prague, to celebrate the tenth anniversary of the independence of Czechoslovakia.

The Czech Republic also has a strong film tradition. In the 1960s, the films of the Czech New Wave, which often focused on everyday life, drew international attention. Jiri Menzel's *Closely Watched Trains* won an Academy Award for Best Foreign Language Film. New Wave director Milos Forman would go on to have a successful career in the United States,

**Antonin Dvorak sometimes wove Bohemian folk melodies into his classical compositions.**

directing films including *One Flew over the Cuckoo's Nest* and *Amadeus*.

## A Rich Music Heritage

Traditional Czech music uses handcrafted wooden instruments such as fiddles, as well as drums and brass instruments like saxophones. Bedrich Smetana became an important composer during the Czech National Revival and is known for his patriotic symphony *Ma vlast* (My Homeland). His contemporary Antonin Dvorak became an internationally renowned classical composer and was the director of the National Conservatory of Music in New York City from 1892 to 1895.

Jazz music was an important part of the underground music scene during the communist era. Jazz singer Karel Gott was a popular figure in the 1960s and 1970s because of his ability to appeal to the younger generation without becoming a target of censorship. In the 1970s, censorship banned the entire genre of rock music, and persecuted rock fans and any musicians whose work resembled that of Western artists. Rock was seen as a symbol of rebellion and free speech, and neither was acceptable to the communists. The members of the rock group the Plastic People of the Universe were among the most out-spoken musicians. They refused to be censored, and they were arrested multiple times.

## A Love of Competition

The Czech enjoy a variety of sports and proudly participate in the Olympic games. Czechs have long excelled in the decathlon, a difficult sport in which athletes compete in ten different

**Jazz musicians perform for passersby on the Charles Bridge in Prague.**

track-and-field events. Czechs have twice brought home the decathlon gold medal: Robert Zmelik in 1992 and Roman Sebrle in 2004.

Thanks to the plentiful mountain rivers, Czech athletes are also among the top water slalom competitors. Lukas Pollert won the gold medal in 1992 and the silver in 1996, and Stepanka Hilgertova won the gold in 1996 and 2000. Volleyball is an increasingly popular sport, and the Czech Republic played a major part in the recent creation of the European Volleyball League.

Many fantastic tennis players have also emerged from what is now the Czech Republic. Martina Navratilova is considered

Martina Navratilova was known for her aggressive playing style.

A woman races down a slope during a ski-bobbing event in the Czech Republic. Ski-bobbing has been a competitive sport in central Europe since the 1950s.

one of the greatest female tennis players ever. She dominated the sport in the late 1970s and 1980s. She won a record nine Wimbledon singles titles, including a phenomenal six in a row. During the same era, Ivan Lendl was the number one male player for five straight years. Current top Czech players include Petra Kvitova and Tomas Berdych.

Ice hockey is considered by many to be the national sport. The men's Olympic team won the gold medal in 1998 and the bronze in 2006. Czech players who have played in the National Hockey League in the United States and Canada include David Krejci, Jakub Voracek, and Jiri Hudler. Other popular winter sports in the Czech Republic include snow tubing, bobsledding, and ski-bobbing. In ski-bobbing, a person races down a snowy hillside sitting on a bicycle-like frame that has skis on the bottom instead of wheels.

# CHAPTER 10

# Life in Czechia

**F**OR MOST CZECH PEOPLE, DAILY LIFE IS SIMILAR TO that of people in the rest of Europe and North America. But there are some differences. Fewer people own cars than in the United States. Public transportation is very good in the Czech Republic and is often the easiest way to get around, with trains and buses offering an affordable option for people in rural areas. Also, cars are much smaller than in the United States. Most SUVs and trucks are driven only for business purposes.

Families tend to be smaller in the Czech Republic as well. The nation has one of the lowest birth rates in the world, with most families having only one child.

*Opposite:* **A mother and daughter take a selfie at a Christmas market in Prague.**

## Education

In the Czech Republic, preschool is viewed as the foundation of a good education. Preschools have class size limits, and all teachers must have a specialized degree to teach.

Primary school is mandatory for children ages six to fifteen. The structure is similar to elementary schools in the United States and Canada, with a class typically spending its day with the same teacher for most subjects. At the end of primary school, all students take a school-leaving examination, a test that shows proficiency in various subjects. The results are used for admission to the next level of school.

Students have many choices for the type of secondary schools they can attend, and their choice will determine their life career path.

**Many Czech schools use computers in the classroom.**

## National Holidays

| | |
|---|---|
| Restoration Day of the Independent Czech State, New Year's Day | January 1 |
| Good Friday | March or April |
| Easter | March or April |
| Labor Day | May 1 |
| Liberation Day | May 8 |
| Sts. Cyril and Methodius Day | July 5 |
| Jan Hus Day | July 6 |
| St. Wenceslas Day (Czech Statehood Day) | September 28 |
| Independent Czechoslovak State Day | October 28 |
| Struggle for Freedom and Democracy Day | November 17 |
| Christmas Eve | December 24 |
| Christmas Day | December 25 |
| St. Stephen's Day | December 26 |

**Carnival celebration in Vortova**

Grammar schools are the most common type of secondary school. These schools focus on general academics and are designed to prepare students for higher education at a university. Many subjects are required, but students are also able to take classes in specific subjects that interest them.

Vocational schools are an option for those who want to learn a specific skill or trade. Students receive a certificate upon completion, and they can then take another examination to apply for additional schooling. Apprenticeship is another option for those who know what career they would

**Students from a music school perform in Prague's Old Town.**

## Unique Schools

In the last few decades, students have been less interested in vocational schools that issue certificates in traditional crafts such as tinsmithing, upholstery, or carpentry. Because of this, vocational schools have begun to tailor their programs to attract students by offering new programs. These new courses help meet the demands of the job market and offer students the chance to become highly specialized in a unique field.

In 2009, the Agricultural Secondary School in Benesov began offering a certificate in golf course

maintenance (above). Though the training is agricultural, it is meeting the needs of the modern tourism industry in the Czech Republic and internationally.

The Artistic Organ Building School in Krnov offers students the opportunity to become masters of the art of instrument making. In addition to organs, students can focus on guitar making and learn to craft fine furniture.

In Horice, students can become experts in stone quarrying and processing (left) at the Sculpture and Stonemasonry School. Once devoted to stonecutting, the school is now the only place in the country to offer studies in the science of quarrying, and graduates are able to find work worldwide in this industry.

Czech university students check out a race car they built. They will race it against cars made by students from other universities.

like. In an apprenticeship, a person gets hands-on training, working with an experienced person in the field.

Lyceums are an optional level of school that provide training in specialized topics at a higher level than vocational schools. They provide an opportunity for students in fields such as engineering, science, medicine, and technology to study their career in depth to obtain additional certifications. Graduates may then choose to begin their careers or continue on to a university where they can earn a professional degree.

Conservatories and artistic schools are an option for those committed to a career in music, dance, dramatics, or fine arts. Admission is based on a talent audition. These schools are very competitive, designed for only the most dedicated students.

## Wedding Traditions

There are many wedding rituals in the Czech Republic, some old, some new. Here are a few:

- Before the reception, a plate is shattered on the floor. The bride and groom must clean it up together to show that they are now partners in all challenges.
- The bride and groom eat soup while bound together and using only one spoon. It represents the cooperation needed in marriage.
- The bride and groom split a loaf of bread in half and present each other with equal parts to symbolize their equality in all things.

- Rice, confetti, nuts, or raisins are tossed at the couple after the ceremony to bring abundance to their new life.
- The groom carries the bride over the threshold of their new home to keep the ghosts that live under the doorstep from waking up.
- Friends and family toss nuts, figs, and coins at the couple in front of their new home as an offering to the ghosts of the house so they will welcome the couple.

## Favorite Foods

Traditional Czech foods are similar to the cuisine of other central and eastern European countries. They tend to be heavy, using abundant meats, starches, and sauces.

Breakfast tends to be simple, often bread with ham, salami, or some other meat. Many people enjoy having something

**Open-faced sandwiches are a common meal in the Czech Republic.**

**A man sells sausages at a market stall.**

sweet as well, such as a sweet bread, a doughnut, or some other pastry. Lunch and dinner are larger and heavier, often featuring meat, potatoes, and soups.

Potatoes are a staple ingredient in Czech cuisine. They are used in soups, or boiled, fried, roasted, or mashed as a side dish. They can be made into dumplings, added to breads, and served cold in salad. Cabbage is also widely used in traditional dishes. Sometimes the cabbage is turned into sauerkraut. Other times it is stewed or used in soup.

Meat is a central part of the day's main meal. Pork is common, often served as a roast or as schnitzel, thinly cut and then breaded and fried. Sausage is also a favorite, cooked

## Mushrooming—A National Sport?

Sometimes referred to as the meat of the poor, mushrooms have long been an important food to the Czech people. Inexpensive, filling, and nutritious, they have become an essential ingredient in many traditional dishes. It is estimated that 70 percent of Czechs go mushroom picking at least once each year, and 20 percent do it regularly. Mushrooms are found in the woods. Being able to identify the edible varieties is very important since some types are poisonous. Czech mushroomers pride themselves on their extensive knowledge and carrying on the longstanding tradition. In Czech folklore, mushrooms bring strength and good health.

**A chef adds the filling to kolaches.**

alone or added to soups and other dishes. Beef is often used alongside pork in sausages, casseroles, and stews. Other traditional dishes feature goose, chicken, pheasant, and rabbit. Soups are served with main meals, and popular varieties feature garlic, sauerkraut, or dumplings. Beef stew, called goulash, is a popular traditional dish.

The national beverage is beer, and it accompanies many meals, although mineral water, milk, fruit juice, and sodas are available everywhere.

Czechs have a sweet tooth, too, and love their desserts. Sweet breads are popular and may be served at any meal. Kolach is a traditional yeast-based sweet

## Zemlovka

Zemlovka is a light bread pudding that makes a perfect dessert. Have an adult help you with this recipe.

### Ingredients

¼ cup raisins

¼ cup finely chopped walnuts

1 teaspoon cinnamon

½ cup + 3 tablespoons sugar

1 ½ cups whole milk, warmed

2 eggs, separated

½ stick melted butter

½ loaf French bread, cut into ¼ inch slices

1 pound apples, peeled and sliced

### Directions

Preheat the oven to 350°F. Prepare an 8 x 8 inch baking dish by coating it in a thin layer of butter. Then mix the raisins, walnuts, cinnamon, and ½ cup sugar and set them aside. Mix the milk, 1 tablespoon sugar, the egg yolks, and melted butter in a shallow bowl. Soak the bread slices in the mixture. Place a single layer of bread slices in the bottom of the baking pan. Add half of the apple slices on the top of the bread layer. Sprinkle half the sugar and spice mixture over the apples. Then add another layer of soaked bread pieces. Repeat with the rest of the apples and sugar and spices. Top with a final layer of soaked bread.

    Beat the egg whites until stiff peaks form, gradually adding 2 tablespoons of sugar. Spread this mixture on top of the dessert, and then bake for 30 minutes. Allow the zemlovka to cool for ten minutes and then serve.

**Trdelnik, spirals of grilled dough usually dusted in cinnamon sugar, are a popular street snack in the Czech Republic.**

bread with filling, resembling a mini open-faced pie. Popular fillings are sweetened poppy seeds, cherries, and nuts with spices. In addition to being a common ingredient in cakes, pies, cookies, and breads, poppy seeds are also added to savory dishes and sauces. Anise and caraway are frequently used to flavor desserts like cookies, cakes, and sweet breads.

Sweet dumplings, often filled with fruit or jam, are a unique Czech dish. Crepes are a favorite dessert and may be filled with almost anything, from butter and sugar to fresh fruit and whipped cream. Apples are used frequently in desserts like strudels, cakes, and bread pudding called zemlovka.

## Out and About

Czech families typically eat in restaurants less often than American families. Many people enjoy socializing out, however. There is nothing Czechs like better than meeting friends at a café or a pub, and spending the evening chatting and laughing. It is the perfect end to a day in the Czech Republic.

**The Czech Republic's welcoming cafés encourage long conversations.**

# Timeline

## CZECH HISTORY

Early people settle at Predmosti. **27,000–24,000 BCE**

A Celtic tribe called the Boii **ca. 4th century BCE**
arrives in the region.

Slavs migrate into the **400–500 CE**
region from the east.

Mojmir establishes the **830**
Great Moravian Empire.

The Premyslid dynasty conquers **907**
the Moravian Empire.

Prince Vratislav becomes the **1085**
first official Czech king.

The Holy Roman Empire issues the **1212**
Golden Bull of Sicily, strengthening
the authority of Bohemian kings.

The Premyslid dynasty ends with **1306**
the murder of King Wenceslas III.

Charles IV begins his long reign, which **1346**
coincides with Prague's Golden Age.

The first Czech university is founded, **1348**
known today as Charles University.

Jan Hus is burned at the stake **1415**
for the crime of heresy against
the Roman Catholic Church.

The Hussite Revolution begins. **1419**

The Compacts of Basel are signed, **1436**
ending the Hussite Revolution and
allowing Protestants to worship
in a Roman Catholic domain.

## WORLD HISTORY

**ca. 2500 BCE** The Egyptians build the pyramids
and the Sphinx in Giza.

**ca. 563 BCE** The Buddha is born in India.

**313 CE** The Roman emperor Constantine
legalizes Christianity.

**610** The Prophet Muhammad begins
preaching a new religion called Islam.

**1054** The Eastern (Orthodox) and Western
(Roman Catholic) Churches break apart.

**1095** The Crusades begin.

**1215** King John seals the Magna Carta.

**1300s** The Renaissance begins in Italy.

**1347** The plague sweeps through Europe.

**1453** Ottoman Turks capture Constantinople,
conquering the Byzantine Empire.

**1492** Columbus arrives in North America.

## CZECH HISTORY

| | |
|---|---|
| Ferdinand I of the Austrian Habsburg family takes over the throne and reinstates Roman Catholicism as the official religion. | **1526** |
| King Matthias begins to oppress Protestants. | **1611** |
| Habsburg armies defeat a Protestant army at the Battle of White Mountain, beginning the Thirty Years' War. | **1620** |
| The Czech language is banned. | **1621** |
| Joseph II's Edict of Toleration restores some religious freedom to Protestants. | **1781** |
| The Czech National Revival begins. | **Late 1700s** |
| The independent state of Czechoslovakia is established. | **1918** |
| German troops invade Czechoslovakia. | **1939** |
| Soviet and U.S. troops liberate Czechoslovakia from Nazi occupation. | **1945** |
| A Soviet-controlled communist government takes over Czechoslovakia. | **1948** |
| Reformers work to increase freedom in the Prague Spring; Soviet forces invade Czechoslovakia to stop the changes. | **1968** |
| The Velvet Revolution ends communist rule. | **1989** |
| Czechoslovakia splits into two independent countries, the Czech Republic and Slovakia; Vaclav Havel becomes the first president of the Czech Republic. | **1993** |
| The Czech Republic joins the European Union. | **2004** |
| The Czech Republic holds its first direct presidential election. | **2013** |

## WORLD HISTORY

| | |
|---|---|
| **1500s** | Reformers break away from the Catholic Church, and Protestantism is born. |
| **1776** | The U.S. Declaration of Independence is signed. |
| **1789** | The French Revolution begins. |
| **1865** | The American Civil War ends. |
| **1879** | The first practical lightbulb is invented. |
| **1914** | World War I begins. |
| **1917** | The Bolshevik Revolution brings communism to Russia. |
| **1929** | A worldwide economic depression begins. |
| **1939** | World War II begins. |
| **1945** | World War II ends. |
| **1969** | Humans land on the Moon. |
| **1975** | The Vietnam War ends. |
| **1989** | The Berlin Wall is torn down as communism crumbles in Eastern Europe. |
| **1991** | The Soviet Union breaks into separate states. |
| **2001** | Terrorists attack the World Trade Center in New York City and the Pentagon near Washington, D.C. |
| **2004** | A tsunami in the Indian Ocean destroys coastlines in Africa, India, and Southeast Asia. |
| **2008** | The United States elects its first African American president. |
| **2016** | Donald Trump is elected U.S. president. |

# Fast Facts

**Official name:** Czech Republic

**Capital:** Prague

**Official language:** Czech

Prague

National flag

Adrspach-Teplice Rocks

| | |
|---|---|
| **Official religion:** | None |
| **Year of founding:** | 1993 |
| **National anthem:** | *"Kde domov muj?"* ("Where Is My Home?") |
| **Type of government:** | Parliamentary republic |
| **Head of state:** | President |
| **Head of government:** | Prime minister |
| **Area of country:** | 30,450 square miles (78,865 sq km) |
| **Latitude and longitude of geographic center:** | 49°45' N, 15°30' E |
| **Bordering countries:** | Germany to the west, Poland to the northeast, Slovakia to the southeast, Austria to the south |
| **Highest elevation:** | Mount Snezka, 5,256 feet (1,602 m) above sea level |
| **Lowest elevation:** | Village of Hrensko, 377 feet (115 m) above sea level |
| **Longest river:** | Vltava, 267 miles (430 km) |
| **Largest lake:** | Black Lake, 45 acres (18 ha) |
| **Average high temperature:** | In Prague, 34°F (1°C) in January, 76°F (24°C) in July |
| **Average low temperature:** | In Prague, 25°F (–4°C) in January, 55°F (13°C) in July |
| **Average annual precipitation:** | 18 to 60 inches (45 to 150 cm), depending on location |

Cesky Krumlov

**National population
(2016 est.):** 10,578,820

**Population of major
cities (2017 est.):**

| | |
|---|---|
| Prague | 1,165,581 |
| Brno | 369,559 |
| Ostrava | 313,088 |
| Pilsen | 164,180 |
| Olomouc | 101,268 |

**Landmarks:**
- ▶ *Cathedral of Sts. Peter and Paul*, Brno
- ▶ *Cesky Krumlov Castle*, Cesky Krumlov
- ▶ *Charles Bridge*, Prague
- ▶ *Prague Castle*, Prague
- ▶ *Spas of Karlovy Vary*, Karlovy Vary

**Economy:** The Czech economy is dominated by the service sector, which employs about 60 percent of the workforce. Machinery and transportation equipment are the most profitable exports. Agriculture accounts for only a small part of the economy. Major products include wheat, sugar beets, barley, hops, cattle, and pigs. Coal accounts for the majority of mined resources.

**Currency:** The Czech koruna. In 2017, 1 koruna equaled US$0.05, and 22 korunas equaled US$1.00.

**System of weights
and measures:** Metric system

**Literacy rate (2012):** 99%

Currency

Schoolchildren

Martina Navratilova

**Common Czech words and phrases:**

| | |
|---|---|
| *Dobry den* | Hello |
| *Na shledanou* | Good-bye |
| *Jak se jmenujete?* | What's your name? |
| *Jak se mate?* | How are you? |
| *Mam se dobre, dekuji.* | I'm fine, thank you. |
| *Mluvite anglicky?* | Do you speak English? |
| *Nemluvim cesky.* | I don't speak Czech. |
| *Kolik je hodin?* | What time is it? |

**Prominent Czechs:**

Zdenek Burian (1905–1981)
*Painter and illustrator*

Karel Capek (1890–1938)
*Writer*

Antonin Dvorak (1841–1904)
*Classical composer*

Vaclav Havel (1936–2011)
*Playwright, political activist, and president*

Jan Hus (ca.1370–1415)
*Early Protestant leader*

Josef Jungmann (1773–1847)
*Father of the modern Czech language*

Franz Kafka (1883–1924)
*Novelist from Prague who wrote in German*

Martina Navratilova (1956–)
*Tennis champion*

# To Find Out More

## Books

- ▶ DK Eyewitness Travel. *Czech and Slovak Republics*. London: DK Eyewitness Travel, 2015.

- ▶ Wisniewski, David. *Golem*. Boston: HMH Books for Young Readers, 2007.

## Music

- ▶ Dvorak, Antonin. *Dvorak: Symphony No. 9*. Berlin: Deutsche Grammophon, 1993.

- ▶ The Plastic People of the Universe. *Musical Nights*. Madrid: Munster Records, 2010.

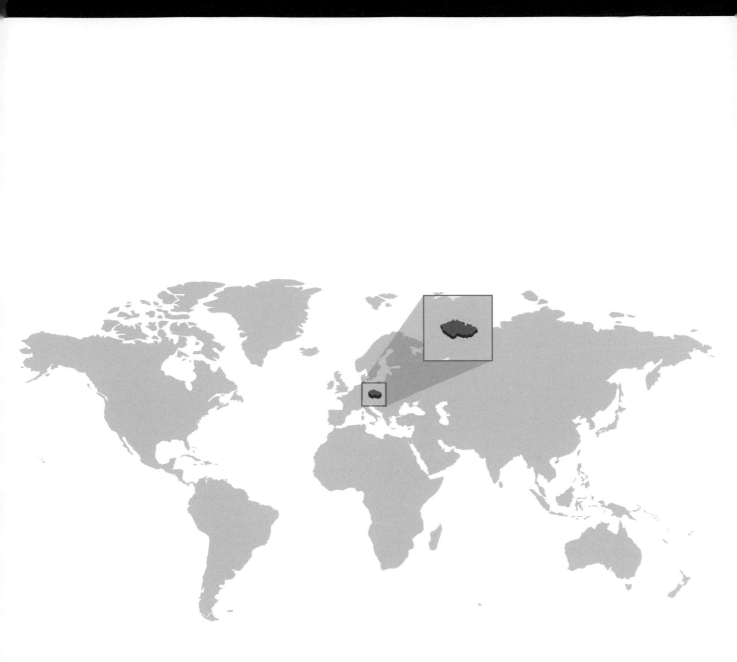

▶ Visit this Scholastic website for more information on the Czech Republic:

**www.factsfornow.scholastic.com**

Enter the keywords **Czech Republic**

# Index

Page numbers in *italics*
indicate illustrations.

# Meet the Author

**L**URA ROGERS SEAVEY STUDIED LIBERAL arts at Skidmore College in New York and Harvard University in Massachusetts where she received her bachelor of arts degree. She has written several other books in the Enchantment of the World series, including *Switzerland, Spain, Dominican Republic,* and *Nigeria.* She is also author of *More Than Petticoats: Remarkable Massachusetts Women,* a collection of short biographies. She enjoys traveling with her two daughters and keeping a small farm.

# Photo Credits